CW01508011

Hilda
of Whitby

The right of Simon Webb to be identified
as the Author of the Work has been asserted by
him in accordance with the Copyright, Designs
and Patents Act 1988.

All rights reserved.

Published by The Langley Press, 2024

Hilda
of Whitby

Simon Webb

Also from the Langley Press

Aidan of Lindisfarne

The Legend of St Cuthbert

In Search of Bede

In Search of the Northern Saints

In Search of the Celtic Saints

For more titles from the Langley Press,
please visit our website at:

www.langleypress.co.uk

Contents

Bede, from the Nuremberg Chronicle, 1493.

Light in a Dark Age

The Yorkshire seaside town of Whitby is famous for five things; its use as a setting in the novel *Dracula*, its whaling history, its jet, its fossils and its saint – Hild or Hilda of Whitby, one of the so-called Northern Saints. The lives of these celebrated holy folk overlapped and, as we shall see, Hilda knew several other local saints personally. Their number includes Aidan, Cuthbert, Wilfrid and Bede, the last of whom is our main source for the life of Hilda. The venerable historian included her biography in his *Ecclesiastical History of the English People*, completed around 731 CE.

Born in the 670s, Bede, who died in 735, would have been around ten years old when Hilda herself died in 680. As a monk as well as a biographer, historian, theologian and scientist, Bede would have had the opportunity of meeting people who remembered Hilda: several times in his *History*, he tells us about people he met who had witnessed the important events and met the notable people about whom he wrote. Bede also had access to documents, some now long lost, that shed light on Hilda's life and background. In his quest to present a detailed picture of the holy history of Britain, Bede cast his net wide, relying on a priest called Nothhelm to ransack archives held at Canterbury and Rome for relevant data. Bede's dogged and well-travelled researcher became Archbishop of Canterbury in the year Bede died, and is now considered a saint in his own right.

Bede, who is buried under the floor of Durham Cathedral's Galilee chapel, could hardly be more prestigious as an author, but as a historian he is not always entirely reliable. Though he wrote about time itself, and championed the BC/AD system of counting the years, he is sometimes wrong about dates, and gives prominence to miracles that even the most devout modern Christian might find unlikely. He confuses legend and history: some of the legends he re-tells look like folksy simplifications of complex events that covered many years and involved thousands of very diverse people. An example would be the gradual invasion of Britain by the Anglo-Saxons (some modern historians would dispute the use of the word 'invasion' here). The legendary accounts tend to boil these events down to dramatic, even melodramatic tales, involving just a few named individuals.

Unlike most of today's academic historians, Bede admitted that he was chiefly concerned with the good influence his history might have on the behaviour of his readers, which implies that he had an agenda other than absolute accuracy. Although he handled various religions, and shades of the Christian religion, in his *Ecclesiastical History*, he was biased towards the so-called Latin Christianity of his own sect, and tended to dismiss what we now call the Celtic Christianity of the Irish missionaries to

England, and the faith of those Britons who still followed the variety of Christianity that had been left behind by the ancient Romans.

Part of Bede's belief-system as revealed through his *Ecclesiastical History* is his conviction that victory in battle is God's reward for the virtue and faithfulness of the victor, whereas failure reflects the corruption and faithlessness to be found in the ranks of the defeated. As it did for Oliver Cromwell centuries later, this idea, which is an important theme in the Old Testament, caused the Anglo-Saxon historian serious problems. Whereas we might say that a victor was just lucky, or brought more troops into the field, Bede feels obliged to cast around for religious reasons why one side won and the other lost.

Bede is also usually more interested in what people did and said, and in their family heritage, than he is in how they looked, whereas now there is a whole industry concerned with using various technologies to recreate the faces of famous figures from the past. As in the Bible, about which Bede wrote so learnedly, the physical reality of a person was usually only of interest to him if it had something to do with their story. The ecclesiastical historian also lacks our modern sense of landscape, and the look of buildings and costumes – the atmospheric descriptions that can make a setting come to life for the reader. Writing for eighth-century European readers, most of whom would have been monks or clerics, it might have seemed superfluous to him to describe in detail, for example, how a bishop dressed in those days: they had all seen several.

Re-examining Bede's approach to Hilda, commentators like Stephanie Hollis have suggested that the historian may have diminished her importance (see Hollis's *Anglo-Saxon Women and the Church: Sharing a Common Fate*). The author of the *Ecclesiastical History* also seems not to have known about a Whitby tradition that links Hilda, in an unexpected way, with the ammonite fossils that are still found in such numbers in the area.

We now know that ammonites are all that is left of ancient sea creatures, similar to the modern nautilus, which died out some sixty-six million years ago. It seems that at some point in the Middle Ages a different explanation arose: that the Whitby ammonites were the remains of snakes that were turned to stone by Saint Hilda. This was the saint's miraculous response to a plague of snakes that was afflicting the town.

Turning living things to stone by magic is an ancient idea: in classical mythology the monster Medusa, usually depicted with snakes instead of hair, turned people to stone just by making herself visible to them. The idea is also re-used in the Narnia novels of C.S. Lewis. In the Judaeo-Christian tradition, snakes are often seen as inherently evil, something that no doubt dates back to Genesis, where Eve is tempted by the subtle serpent. That snakes needed to be controlled by saints or other good Christians seems to have been a given for medieval Christians. The absence of native Irish snakes (something Ireland shares with the Hawaiian islands) was traditionally explained with the story that St Patrick banished them all, at which point they wriggled off into the sea.

In an Anglo-Saxon book of saints in which Hilda and other Northern Saints make appearances, we learn about Anatolia, an Italian saint of the third century, who was locked up in a cell with a venomous snake – identified in the Old English source as an adder. But Anatolia tamed the snake, which even bowed to her when she bowed to it, and did not offer to bite her. Audax, the man who had brought the snake along in the first place, was so impressed that he became a Christian convert, and died a saint himself (see *An Old English Martyrology*, ed. George Herzfeld).

As well as snakes, saints and other heroes are often associated with the control or destruction of mythical reptiles such as dragons, often called, in the English tradition, 'worms'. The most famous dragon-killing saint is of course George, a fourth-century saint from what is now Turkey. Another fourth-century dragon-slaying saint who came from part of what we now call Turkey was Margaret of Antioch, whom some say killed her dragon in the messiest way possible. She was swallowed by her worm, but was too holy to stay long in his digestive system. The poor beast burst open, and she was able to climb out unhurt.

If one is unable to believe such stories, one might opt to accept them as symbolic tales about the battle of good and evil, and the triumph of light over darkness. Certainly Hilda's time was a dark one in many respects. Much violence and slaughter were caused by the conflicts between the indigenous British or Celtic occupants of Britain, and Hilda's people, the Anglo-Saxons, who by her time had been steadily taking over their territory for centuries.

According to Bede, Hilda, child of this benighted time, was associated with light even when she was a small child. While she was still an infant, Hilda's mother Bregusuid had one of those vexatious dreams in which one is hunting for a person, place or item that cannot be found. In Bregusuid's case, that which was lost was her husband, Hilda's father Hereric, who was missing both in her dream and in real life. After searching fruitlessly in her dream, Hilda's mother noticed a necklace glowing under her garments, that shone so brightly that it seemed to fill the whole of Britain with its light. This Bregusuid took to be a portent of the later sanctity of her daughter. Somehow, it seems, Hilda's mother understood that the glowing necklace represented her younger daughter, Hilda, not Hilda's older sister, Hereswith.

Sigmund Freud or one of his modern-day followers might interpret Bregusuid's dream as a reflection of her psychological plight after she learned of the death of her husband. Now unable to have more children by him, the children she had were even more precious to her. This might have bred an unhealthy, smothering relationship between mother and child, but Hilda's later success and the esteem she won from everyone suggests that Bregusuid's parenting was more about encouragement than suffocation.

The reason why Bregusuid was hunting so anxiously for her husband in a dream was because he was absent from home at the time, living as a banished man in the court of Cerdic (or Ceretic), King of the Britons of Loidis and Elmet. Loidis is now called Leeds, and Elmet was a separate kingdom straddling what we now call Yorkshire and Derbyshire. That Hereric, evidently an Anglo-Saxon, was living as an exile at the court of a king of the Britons or Celts is intriguing.

Bede tells us that Hereric was a nephew of King Edwin of Northumbria, which makes Edwin Hilda's great-uncle. Both Edwin and Hereric had been forced to find somewhere to live outside of their native kingdoms, because they were enemies, or perceived enemies, of Aethelfrith, Edwin's predecessor as King of Northumbria. Aethelfrith had started off, around 592 AD, as King of Bernicia, the half of Northumbria that lay north of the mouth of the River Tees, but around 604 he became King of Deira to the south as well, thus uniting Northumbria into one kingdom. It was as members of the Deiran royal family that Edwin and his nephew Hereric were forced to flee. It was in 604, by the way, that Pope Gregory the Great, for whom the Christianisation of the English was a pet project, died in Rome at the age of sixty-three or sixty-four. According to some sources, it was also in this year or the year before that the Roman Senate last met in Rome itself.

Hereric may have looked for help to a Celtic king on the basis that 'the enemy of my enemy is my friend'. It turned out, however, that Hilda's father was not safe at the court of the King of Loidis and Elmet. He was poisoned there, though who poisoned him and why are questions that cannot be answered with any certainty. Had agents of Aethelfrith poisoned him, or had Cerdic been bribed and/or threatened into giving Hereric a deadly draught? It is possible, or course, that Cerdic had poisoned his Anglo-Saxon guest on his own account and for his own reasons.

The fate of Hilda's father Hereric offers a glimpse into the brutality of her age. Not only were there endless wars between the Anglo-Saxons and their rivals the Celts or Britons: the Anglo-Saxons fought each other.

Saxon nun, from an eighteenth-century book on costume.

Hilda's People

Whoever was responsible for her father's poisoning, Hereric's death meant that Hilda and her mother either remained at the court of King Edwin, or went there seeking his protection. Edwin would have been in his late twenties when Hilda was born: he replaced Aethelfrith as King of Northumbria in about the year 616 (the year of the death of Aethelfrith) when Edwin would have turned thirty, and Hilda was only about two years old.

One reason why the Saxon kings warred against each other and against the Celts was to gain more territory. Bede tells us that as a king Edwin was so successful that he gained control of every part of Britain; Celtic and Saxon, south and north of the River Humber (the northern part being Northumbria) with the possible exception of Kent. Edwin even managed to conquer the Isle of Man, which is probably the island Bede means by the name 'Mevania'. Bede assures us that Edwin was the first to dominate Britain to such an extent, and, true to form, attributes his victories to his personal virtue.

Although Hilda became a Christian saint, if she spent her childhood at the court of King Edwin then she was in effect raised as a pagan. Little is known about the paganism of the Anglo-Saxons – the religion they brought with them from their Germanic and Scandinavian homelands. According to Bede, the ancestors of the likes of Edwin and Hilda began to arrive in Britain, along with their gods, after 449, over a century and a half before the latter was born, and some forty years after the Romans had finally abandoned the British Isles.

We get a glimpse of life in the homelands of the Anglo-Saxons from the *Germania* of Tacitus, written about a century after the birth of Jesus. The Roman historian notes the cold blue eyes of the Germans, and their reddish hair. He assumes that theirs is a very pure race, unmixed with foreign blood, because getting to Germany to invade or settle it would be problematic, given the turbulent character of the North Sea. Tacitus also suggests that this thickly forested land would not attract newcomers in any case, since it is so cold and grim.

The Roman historian admires the Germans for their hardiness and courage in war, and notices other elements of their culture that may have a bearing on our understanding of Hilda. In certain ceremonies and political events among the Germans, the (pagan) priests held sway and had to be obeyed at all costs. The German women were also noted for their loyalty to their husbands, and their abstention from sex before marriage. Women were regarded as holy creatures possessing prophetic powers: their advice was actively sought, and listened to with attention. Focusing on a subgroup of the Germans whom he calls the Anglii, Tacitus details their devotion to the goddess Nerthus, or Mother Earth. The Roman also noted how the Germans would never hold certain meetings except on days when the phase of the moon seemed auspicious.

A habit of Tacitus's Germans that was definitely followed by the Anglo-Saxons who came to Britain was their preference for houses and other buildings built not of stone but of wood daubed with a kind of plaster. In their German homelands in the time of Tacitus, tribes like the Angles may indeed have been living in clearings in vast primaeval forests that would have given them wood for their buildings, but recent archaeology suggests that this was not the landscape they found in Great Britain. There were certainly vast forests, with bears and wolves lurking among the trees, but there was also a long tradition of farming on land that had been carved out of genuine primaeval forest thousands of years before before the first Angles set foot on the territory that was to be named after them.

As well as well-tilled fields, another sight that would have greeted the Anglo-Saxons as they stepped ashore would have been Roman remains, some of them in much better condition than they are now. These would have included forts, temples, churches, villas, signal-stations, roads and of course Hadrian's Wall, parts of which have remained visible above ground ever since it was built.

A sense of the Anglo-Saxons' feelings about the ghosts of Rome that they came to live amongst can be gleaned from the Old English poem *The Ruin*. This is usually taken to be a description of then-surviving Roman buildings in the city of

Bath. *The Ruin* evokes a picture of the poet standing reverently by a broken stone wall, trying to imagine how the builders of the wall had lived.

The Anglo-Saxons who were the descendants of some of Tacitus's Germans are supposed to have been invited over by a British king called Vortigern, who hoped to be able to employ them as mercenaries to fight off the various invaders of what became England. The invaders, who included both Irish adventurers and Picts from what we now call Scotland, were emboldened by the fact that Great Britain south of Hadrian's Wall was no longer defended by Roman legions, who had once guarded the coast and patrolled the Wall.

To the sceptical reader, Vortigern feels like a legendary or semi-legendary figure, perhaps based on the real ruler of some part of beleaguered Britain who is otherwise lost in time. Bede's mention of him is an example of his use of legends that simplify and dramatise complex events. Modern studies suggest that the beginning of the Saxon invasion of Britain must have involved far more than just one king inviting a small group of Saxon mercenaries to serve under him. Some of the Germanic newcomers would not have been invaders at all, but merely settlers in unpopulated lands.

In Bede's account, the Saxon mercenaries looked around and realised that they had arrived in a large, fertile country that was poorly defended. More came, so many from the country of the Angles (on the border of modern Germany and Denmark) that according to Bede their continental home became an empty wilderness. The spread of the Angles, Saxons, Jutes and Frisians across Britain was probably another of those complex phenomena that the people of

Bede's time had to simplify to understand. Bede tells us that the newcomers waged many wars against the Britons, who had become lazy, decadent and sinful because of the easy living that a series of bumper harvests had given them. Working in league with the Picts who were among the people they had originally been brought over to fight, the Saxons carried all before them. In the words of A.M. Sellar's translation of Bede's *Ecclesiastical History*:

Public as well as private buildings were overturned; the priests were everywhere slain before the altars; no respect was shown for office, the prelates with the people were destroyed with fire and sword; nor were there any left to bury those who had been thus cruelly slaughtered. Some of the miserable remnant, being taken in the mountains, were butchered in heaps. Others, spent with hunger, came forth and submitted themselves to the enemy, to undergo for the sake of food perpetual servitude, if they were not killed upon the spot. Some, with sorrowful hearts, fled beyond the seas. Others, remaining in their own country, led a miserable life of terror and anxiety of mind among the mountains, woods and crags.

(From Chapter XV)

Bede's source for this horrific account of Saxon war-crimes was a book called *On the Ruins of Britain* (*De Excidio et Conquestu Britanniae*) written in Latin by a man called Gildas, perhaps two hundred years before Bede completed his *Ecclesiastical History*. Because Gildas was a Briton and not a Saxon like Bede, he felt free to cast rather more shade on the Saxon invaders than the later historian. He called them (as translated by J.A. Giles) 'wolves . . . the fierce and impious Saxons, a race hateful both to God and men'.

If the Christian God hated these 'whelps', the 'bastard-born' Saxons, they reciprocated by attacking both churches and churchmen, so that the streets were littered with the remains of 'holy altars, fragments of human bodies, covered with livid clots of coagulated blood'. It is hardly surprising that the warlike Saxons showed no respect for the status of Christian clergy, as the aggressors were not Christians themselves.

As the pagan invaders spread over the country, they left the names of their gods in various place-names that are still used. These include Tuesley in Surrey, a name presumably derived from that of the warlike god Týr; Wednesbury in Staffordshire (from Woden) and Thursley, also in Surrey, from Thunor or Thor. These place-names derived from the names of the Germanic gods of the Saxons are reminiscent of our English names for three of the days of the week. Another example is Friday, named for the goddess Frig.

For generations historians have used place-names to track the spread of the Anglo-Saxons west across the island of Great Britain. A recent DNA study confirmed many of their findings (see the journal Nature Communications, January 2016). In their report, Stephan Schiffels *et al* showed that whereas some English people living in the east of the island have around thirty-eight percent Anglo-Saxon DNA, this went down to thirty percent in modern Welsh and Scottish people. The investigators established what Anglo-Saxon DNA was like by extracting samples from bodies found in Anglo-Saxon grave sites in Cambridgeshire.

As the Saxons increased the amount of land they controlled, Britain was paganized, or perhaps we should say re-paganized. Gildas recalls how his own Christian Britons had once been pagans, though he refuses to go into detail on this subject. He will not:

> . . . enumerate those diabolical idols of my country, which almost surpassed in number those of Egypt, and of which we still see some mouldering away within or without the deserted temples, with stiff and deformed features as was customary. Nor will I call out upon the mountains, fountains, or hills, or upon the rivers, which now are subservient to the use of men, but once were an abomination and destruction to them, and to which the blind people paid divine honour.

Both Bede and Gildas tell tales of the battles where the Britons beat the Saxons, but neither mentions King Arthur, the legendary hero who is supposed to have routed the Germanic intruders, despite his problem family. Their equivalent of Arthur is the brave Ambrosius Aurelianus, an aristocratic Roman who began to prevail against the invaders and won a decisive battle at Badon Hill near Bath, which checked the Saxon advance for a time. It is only later historians who mention Arthur in connection with this battle.

While Edwin and his kingdom based north of the Humber persisted in their paganism, the kingdom of Kent, which was not part of his empire, had started to become Christian after the arrival of St Augustine of Canterbury in 597 CE, over twenty years before Hilda was born. Augustine had been sent by Pope Gregory I, known as Gregory the Great, for whom, as we know, the Christianisation of the pagan Anglo-Saxons had become a pet project.

Perhaps the most famous story from Bede's *Ecclesiastical History* concerns Gregory's first encounter with Angles. Before he was pope, Gregory spotted some boys 'of fair complexion, with pleasing countenances, and very beautiful hair' offered for sale in the slave-market in Rome. Asking who they were, he was told that they were Angles, and, in a punning mood, remarked that they looked like angels. Told that they came from a kingdom called Deira, Gregory made another pun about the anger (*ira* in Latin) of God. When he learned that the king of that place was called Aelle, the future pope cried out 'Allelujah, the praise of God the Creator must be sung in those parts'.

The earliest extant stand-alone biography of Gregory was penned not in Rome but at Whitby Abbey, a religious house that may have been founded by Hilda herself. The Life, written by an anonymous monk or nun of Whitby early in the eighth century, suggests that Aelle, the name of the Anglian king mentioned in the slave-market story, was a fortuitous pun on the Christian Trinity.

Gregory set out on his own mission to the Angles, but after just four days of travelling he was called back by the pope. He was such a capable and valuable young man that it seems that the people of Rome did not feel that they could do without him. He felt obliged to obey the pontiff's demand that he return, because while he was resting on his journey a locust settled on the Bible he was reading. He cried out 'locusta', which reminded his punning brain of the Latin term '*loco sta*', meaning, 'stay where you are'. In the Whitby Life of Gregory the would-be missionary receives even more encouragement to turn back: here we are told that groups of

Romans arranged themselves at points along Gregory's route and, as he passed, cried out to him to turn back.

If Hilda ever heard the story of Gregory's encounter with the Anglian boys in the slave market, it is likely to have had a personal resonance for her. King Aelle of Deira was her great-grandfather. Although in the Roman slave-market Gregory is supposed to have encountered Angles from Deira in the north, the mission he sent to Britain, led by the monk Augustine, landed at Thanet and began preaching to the court of Ethelbert, the King of Kent. Augustine and his followers had hesitated in their journey and decided to turn back; terrified, perhaps, by the fearsome reputation of the warlike pagan Saxons. But a letter from Pope Gregory rallied their spirits and they completed their journey.

King Ethelbert of Kent was able to understand the Roman missionaries with the help of the interpreters they had brought over with them from the kingdom of the Franks, then roughly equivalent to modern France. The Kentish king was by no means unacquainted with Christianity, since his wife Bertha was a Christian Frank, though he was sufficiently suspicious of his visitors to meet them first in the open air, since there any spells they might try to cast on him would be less effective than they would be indoors. Four years after Augustine arrived in 597, Pope Gregory sent over more missionaries, among them a man called Paulinus.

Gregory did not just send waves of missionaries to the pagan English: he also sent gifts and letters. One of his more interesting epistles was sent in 601, and was copied out by Bede into his *Ecclesiastical History*. It advises an abbot called Mellitus:

. . . that the temples of the idols in that nation [i.e. the English] ought not to be destroyed; but let the idols that are in them be destroyed; let water be consecrated and sprinkled in the said temples, let altars be erected, and relics placed there . . . and because they are accustomed to slaughter many oxen in sacrifice to devils, some celebration must be given them in exchange for this . . . [on Christian holy days they should] kill cattle and glorify God in their feast, and return thanks to the Giver of all things . . . for there is no doubt that it is impossible to cut off every thing at once from their rude natures; because he who endeavours to ascend to the highest place rises by degrees or steps, and not by leaps.

One is reminded of the prophet Muhammad ordering the removal of over three hundred pagan artefacts from the Kaaba in 630 CE (when Hilda would have been a teenager). Something similar can still be seen in Rome itself, where archaeologists have confirmed that long ago churches were built on the sites of pagan temples, and where the Pantheon, built as a temple to all the Roman gods, has now been used as a church for over fourteen centuries. This attitude of Gregory and his missionaries may explain why some very pagan elements still survive in the English language and the customs of the English. We call Easter, that most important of the Christian festivals, by a pagan name, and we still associate mistletoe – sacred to the Druids and other pagans – with Christmas.

A more aggressive example of the re-use of a pagan site is recorded in the biography of St Boniface, who may have been born in Devon in the late 670s. During his missionary work in Germany, he came across a sacred oak dedicated to

Woden. When the saint ordered it to be cut down, the local pagans protested, but the tree miraculously collapsed in a heap after the axe had kissed it just a few times. Impressed, the assembled pagans began to worship the Christian god, and Boniface had an oratory built from the wood of the old tree.

In his letter about the re-purposing of pagan temples Gregory showed some sensitivity about the needs of Anglo-Saxon pagans recently thrown into the new world of Christianity, and perhaps missing their old festivals and wanting to re-visit their ancient pagan shrines. Gregory was not always so sensitive: he approved the use of violence to convince people to convert, under certain circumstances.

While for the English Christianity was something fresh and new, it had been a force in Gregory's Mediterranean world for so long that in some places it had fallen into decadence and corruption. Gregory, a great letter-writer, was for ever corresponding with bishops and others reminding them that they were not supposed to, for instance, order their servants to spend Sunday morning stealing harvest-ready crops from their neighbours. The energetic pope heard that the elderly Bishop Januarius of Cagliari in Sardinia had done this, and was also charging exorbitant fees for Christian burials. Another bishop, Natalis of Salona, had become notorious for the huge banquets he enjoyed. Gregory advised him to eat no more than was 'necessary for refreshing the weakness of the body that it may be kept in health for the practice of virtue' (from Barmby, J., *Gregory the Great*).

More serious were what Gregory regarded as the erroneous and even heretical theological ideas that some

Latin Christians in Europe and beyond continued to believe in, despite official papal disapproval. Many nations, such as the Lombards, who were overrunning large parts of Europe at the time, stubbornly followed their own heretical 'take' on Christianity. Those Lombards who were not pagans adhered to an Arian approach to Christianity: the Arians understood the Trinity in a way that was not consistent with papal teaching, insisting on a greater degree of separation between God the Father and his son, Jesus.

While the Arians had their own ideas about the relationship between God and Jesus, the Nestorian Christians disagreed with the papacy about the nature of Jesus himself. Some thought that certain writings of three fifth-century bishops were Nestorian: the prelates in question were Theodore of Mopsuestia, Theodoret of Cyrus and Ibas of Edessa. The writings that sparked the controversy were known collectively as the Three Chapters (both Mopsuestia and Edessa are now in Turkey).

It is tempting to compare Pope Gregory, who ascended to Peter's chair in 590, and among many other things worked hard to discredit the Three Chapters, with Hilda of Whitby. Both were from powerful patrician families, and both entered religious orders when, as rich entitled youngsters, there were many other options open to them. Both Hilda and Gregory were also called to centres of power against their wills, since both, it seems, really preferred the modest quiet of the cloister.

Hilda was unlike Gregory in that whereas the latter was struggling with paganism at a distance, his own family having been Christian for some time, Hilda was brought up with it and must have seen the signs of it everywhere.

Although Gregory may indeed have had an emotional attachment to the idea of clearing paganism out of the minds of the pale-skinned Anglo-Saxons, he was a diplomat and a politician as well as a scholar and a religious leader, and he may have seen in distant Britain a place into which he could extend his influence and which might, in time, form part of his power-base. In Rome and the Mediterranean world in general, his power was compromised by the fact that in those days there was still a Roman emperor, one who ruled not from Rome itself but from Constantinople, a city re-founded as the eastern capital of the empire by the emperor Constantine (died 337 CE). Since the Romans had abandoned Britain around 410 CE, the emperors who ruled from Constantine's new capital in Gregory's day could hardly claim these islands as part of their bailiwick.

Another reason why Gregory may have turned his eyes to the wild far north-west of Europe was because of the devastation he saw all around him, particularly in Rome. The concentration of imperial power in Constantinople made Rome to a great extent an irrelevance, despite its historic prestige. Much of the city lay in ruins, the population was a small fraction of what it had once been, and crops were being grown and animals grazed where there had once been grand urban spaces. In his first sermon as supreme pontiff Gregory waxed apocalyptic, saying:

Every day the earth is visited by fresh calamities. You see how few remain of the ancient population; each day sees us chastened by fresh afflictions, and unforeseen blows strike us to the ground. The world grows old and hoary, and through a sea of troubles hastens to approaching death.

(from Gregorovius: History of the City of Rome in the Middle Ages, Vol. II, trans. Hamilton)

Gregory's grim sermon was delivered at a time when Rome was under siege by the warlike Lombards, and by plague. There would continue to be an emperor ruling from what had been the Greek city of Byzantium (now Istanbul in Turkey) until the city fell to the Ottoman Turks in 1453. But the authority of the Roman popes over the religion of the Byzantine Greeks of the east ended when the Greek and Roman Churches split away from each other in 1054.

Ammonite – photo by Daderot.

Edwin and Paulinus

According to Bede, Paulinus's relationship with Edwin, the powerful King of Northumbria, dated from before he was king. The story of their first encounter is, however, mysterious, and includes supernatural elements. In the year 616, when his predecessor Ethelfrid died, but before Edwin himself became king, Hilda's great-uncle was in exile in the kingdom of Readwald, King of East Anglia.

Since 1939, when the Sutton Hoo ship burial was uncovered in Suffolk, Readwald has been of rather more interest to historians and archaeologists than he was before. It is possible that it was the body of this fascinating king of East Anglia who was placed under a shelter on the deck of that wooden ship, surrounded by awe-inspiring treasures, some time in the 620s. Once everything was in place, the ship and its passenger to the afterlife were buried under tons of earth, forming the prominent mound that attracted the attention of the twentieth-century investigators.

If the lifeless Sutton Hoo passenger really was Readwald, then he was surely a very rich, powerful and influential king, respected so much after his death that his family and followers were prepared to leave in his grave not just a useable sea-going ship but also some of the most gorgeous jewellery ever produced. Some of the Sutton Hoo treasures had come from distant places like Alexandria in Egypt and the workshops of the Byzantine Empire.

Though they are undeniably impressive, and made with mind-boggling ingenuity, many of the Sutton Hoo treasures are essentially barbaric. Ceremonial swords and ornate parade helmets are the artefacts of a people obsessed with war, much of whose culture was based around preparation for battle. It is possible that the Sutton Hoo helmet, which seems to greet visitors to the British Museum with a baleful glare, was even worn in battle, since it was strongly-made, with an iron core. It may even have been damaged in battle, as a piece that was perhaps used to repair it does not quite match the rest.

There is evidence in the epic Welsh poem *Y Gododdin,* an account of a clash between Celts and Saxons that took place around 600 CE, that the battle equipment of warriors was indeed adorned with gold. This is also an aspect of *The Battle of Maldon*, an Old English poem about Saxons fighting Vikings. The poem gives a vivid picture of warfare at the time. The English chiefs ride to battle on their horses, but fight on foot. Arrows are shot and javelins thrown, then everyone gets down to hand-to-hard combat. Thrusting-spears clash on round shields, and there is some swordplay, while hungry raptors circle overhead. When an English king falls, some from his side ride away, but others, remembering the drunken boasts they had previously made about their prowess in battle, would rather die. Regarding the splendid accoutrements of their opponents, many dream of looting their bodies.

Despite the evident wealth of Readwald's court, the king of the East Angles was still tempted by the bribes offered by Edwin's enemy, King Ethelfrid of the newly-united Northumbria. The king in the distant north was offering a great deal in return for the life of Edwin, who would become his successor. In Bede's account, Ethelfrid tried not just the carrot but also the stick; threatening to make war on Readwald if he did not promptly do away with his princely guest, or at least give him up to some representatives of the Northumbrian king.

At length, Readwald caved in and agreed to either kill Edwin or deliver him to Ethelfrid's goons. A friend of Edwin's heard about this, and found him making ready for bed. He warned the Deiran that his life was in imminent danger, and added that he, the friend, was prepared to help him escape, 'and lead you to a place where neither Readwald nor Ethelfrid shall ever find you'.

Edwin's reply was surprising. He thanked his friend for the warning, but added, 'I cannot go with you: I cannot be the first one to break the compact I have made with this great king. As yet, he has done me no harm, or moved against me at all. If I must die, I had rather he did it than a lesser man. Anyway, where can I go? I have been a fugitive for too many years, wandering through the whole of Britain'.

His friend left Edwin alone, and the prince went outside and sat on a stone within view of Readwald's palace. He sat there a long time, sad and bewildered. It was now the dead of night, and he saw someone approaching. He did not recognise the man, or the type of clothes he wore. The stranger approached, and asked Edwin what he was doing there, alone, awake and anxious.

'What is that to you?' asked Edwin.

'I know why you are sitting here,' said the strange man, 'and who you are, and the evils you fear, and why you are so sad. But tell me,' he went on, 'what reward you would give a man who delivered you out of these troubles, and persuaded Readwald to spare you?'

'A man like that,' said Edwin; 'I would give him everything I could.'

'And what if he could also assure you, that your enemies will be destroyed, and that you will become a king more powerful than all your own ancestors, and all the old kings of the English?'

Edwin repeated his reply to the stranger's first question.

'This man,' the stranger went on, 'if his prophecies turned out to be correct, and he offered to give you better advice than any of your ancestors have had, including the ones who were kings, would you listen to his advice, and follow it?'

'Of course,' said Edwin; 'I would always follow his advice, since he had saved me from so many calamities. I would even make such a man a king in his own right!'

At this answer, the stranger placed his right hand on Edwin's head, and said, 'When you see this sign again, remember our conversation – and remember what you have promised!' With that, Edwin's strange visitor vanished into thin air. The future King of Northumbria decided that he must have met a spirit, and not a human being at all.

Edwin continued to sit on his stone under the stars, until the friend who had offered to smuggle him away from Readwald's court appeared again. 'Get up,' he said, 'and go back inside. Now you can sleep safely. The king has changed his mind – now he will not break his promise to you. He told the queen that he meant to give in to Ethelfrid's demands, and she told him that he should not dishonour himself, just for gold.'

In fact, Readwald's whole policy regarding Edwin now changed. When Ethelfrid's messengers had returned home, Readwald and Edwin set off together at the head of an army, and clashed with Ethelfrid's hastily-assembled forces by the River Idle in what is now Nottinghamshire. There Ethelfrid was slain as well as, tragically, Readwald's son Raegenheri. The king's fallen son may have been buried in the Anglo-Saxon cemetery at Sutton Hoo, but his cannot have been the grand ship-burial that yielded up such rich treasures in 1939. Some of the coins buried under that mound date from the 620s, some years after the Battle of the River Idle.

Following the battle where his enemy Ethelfrid was slain, Edwin was able to seize the kingdom of Northumbria, and become its new king. He was, however, subject to the authority of his patron, champion and saviour Readwald, and ruled his northern kingdom for a time as a sort of puppet monarch. He was perhaps thirty when he ascended the throne and assembled his own court, in which his great-niece Hilda and her mother Bregusuid found shelter. In 625, when he was nearing forty, Edwin married his second wife Ethelburg, a princess from the Christian kingdom of Kent, who was perhaps in her mid-twenties at the time of their marriage. One of the conditions of their marriage was that Edwin should abandon his paganism and embrace the Christian faith. His bride brought with her Paulinus, one of the missionaries sent over by Gregory the Great, who by this time may have been a bishop.

Edwin hesitated over his conversion, despite the fact that he now had a Christian wife, and despite the efforts of Paulinus to convince him. At last Paulinus, whom Edwin seems not to have recognised at first, came to the Northumbrian king and laid his right hand on his head. 'Do you know this sign?' he asked. The king began to tremble. Yes, it had been Paulinus who had visited him, like a spirit, or the ghost of a person still alive, as he sat in the darkness outside Readwald's palace.

'Behold,' said Paulinus, 'by the gift of God you have escaped the hands of the enemies you feared. Thanks to God, you have obtained the kingdom you desired. Make sure you do not delay the fulfilment of your third promise; accept the faith, and keep the precepts of the one who, delivering you from adversity in this world, has raised you to the honour of a worldly kingdom. If, from this time forward, you obey his will, which through me he signifies to you, he will also save you from the everlasting torments of the wicked, and make you a partaker of his eternal kingdom in heaven.'

One would have thought that King Edwin would have converted to Christianity straight away, after this startling conversation with Paulinus. The missionary had shown him that through the power of his God a living man could appear as a spirit to someone far away, and in his speech he had emphasised what God had already done for Edwin, and would do in future. No doubt Edwin's Christian queen would also have like to have seen her husband undergo a kind of emergency baptism, but still his majesty hesitated.

Of course he would now be baptised, but first he would call a meeting of his chief friends and counsellors, to hear what they knew and thought about Christianity, to see if it would be possible for all of them to consent to be baptised at once. First to speak at the meeting was Coifi, the chief of Edwin's pagan priests, who admitted that he had come to believe that their old religion had never been of much use. He complained:

. . . none of your people has applied himself more diligently to the worship of our gods than I; and yet there are many who receive greater favours from you, and are more preferred than I, and are more prosperous in all that they undertake to do or to get.

Coifi's complaint is interesting because he equates success and the good life generally, which he feels he is being denied, with closeness to the king, and bathing in the monarch's favour. Surely, if Woden and the rest were any good, then I, their hard-working follower, would have more luck? Coifi concluded that if further investigation proved that Christianity was better, then they should all convert as soon as possible.

Another of the king's chief men gave a speech which is now famous, and is one of the highlights of Bede's *Ecclesiastical History*. In it he likened life to a warm, bright time spent in the king's great hall while all around is cold and darkness. Our souls, he implied, are like sparrows who fly into the hall 'while the fire blazes in the midst'. The bird tarries a short time, then is out again into the darkness, where 'the wintry storms of rain or snow are raging.

'So this life of man appears for a little while,' the speaker concluded, 'but of what is to follow or what went before we know nothing at all. If, therefore, this new doctrine tells us something more certain, it seems justly to deserve to be followed'.

Again the courtier equates time spent with the king with true felicity, and, as elsewhere in Bede, there are thoughts of death and fear of what it will bring. In the harsh world of the Anglo-Saxons, few people lived very long, and the threat of an early death due to disease or violence was ever-present. Time and again, the *Ecclesiastical History* presents Christianity as a way to in effect cheat death, and enjoy eternal life.

A vivid Anglo-Saxon view of the reality of death and the evanescent nature of life is conveyed in an Anglo-Saxon text included in a manuscript book kept at the Bodleian Library at Oxford, called Bodley 343. Here the anonymous author advises his readers or listeners to pause by the grand tombs of the wealthy dead and reflect that they were as subject to death as any pauper. If the dead could speak to us out of their tombs, they would say, 'I once was as you are now, and you will yet become what I now am' (from Boenig, R, *Anglo-Saxon Spirituality*).

The warm, bright life of the Anglo-Saxon royal hall that is glimpsed so briefly by the sparrow, and used by Edwin's courtier as a metaphor for life itself, was an important part of Anglo-Saxon existence. In the typical royal settlement there would be a large central hall built mainly of wood, surrounded by separate buildings used as kitchens, latrines, workshops and family houses. The immediate followers of the king or local 'thegn' might sleep somewhere in the hall, and this is where political meetings, diplomatic receptions, meals and drinking-bouts would take place. Here also magnificent gifts would be given, and entertainers such as harpists and reciters of poetry would perform.

The world of the royal hall is evoked in the celebrated anonymous Anglo-Saxon epic poem *Beowulf*, based on what was probably an old story passed down in the oral tradition, but written down in the late tenth or early eleventh century. Here Heorot, the grand hall of King Hrothgar, which even has gold as part of its architecture, is threatened by the monster Grendel. Only Beowulf, a mighty warrior of the Geats, can slay the beast.

In the face of the general approval of the new religion expressed by Edwin's courtiers, the old idols and temples were pulled down or burned, Coifi himself acting as the leading arsonist. This may not have been in contravention of Gregory the Great's idea that pagan temples should be re-used, since the celebrated pope had suggested that only the well-built ones should be favoured in this way.

The anonymous Life of Gregory the Great that was written at Whitby early in the eighth century supplies a further episode where Edwin hesitates over his conversion to Christianity. Told very much from the English point of view, this earliest extant biography of the celebrated pope mentions Paulinus many times, as a disciple of Gregory and one of his great gifts to the English. The anonymous author tells us that as the king and his thegns were proceeding to a church to be catechised (or taught the Christian basics) a crow cawed his protest, which the Saxons took as a bad omen. Paulinus called for the bird to be shot with an arrow, then showed the grisly sight of dead bird transfixed with the arrow to his catechumens. If the bird didn't even know that its call would cause its own death, how can you believe it could prophesy anything, Paulinus asked.

As told by Bede, it seems as if the pagan Northumbrians gave up their ancient faith remarkably easily. This was certainly not the case everywhere. The Frankish emperor Charlemagne, who was born nearly twenty years after Bede completed his *History*, used war as a (largely effective) means of spreading the Christian faith. Among those who stood out stubbornly against him were the pagan Saxons who had remained in their German homeland. When they were baptised, the Saxons were required to state that they had forsaken 'all the works and words of the devils, Thor and Woden and Saxnote and all the fiends that are their companions' (from Davies, Owen, *Paganism*). Charlemagne even set up a special 'Capitulary for the Saxon Regions' that prescribed the death penalty for people who returned to pagan practices such as cremating their dead.

Despite perhaps thousands of years of pagan tradition both on the Continent and in Britain, on Easter Sunday 627 there was a mass baptism of Northumbrians in a hastily-constructed church at York: among those baptised was King

Edwin's great-niece Hilda, who would have been a young teenager at the time.

1960s reconstruction of the Sutton Hoo mask.

After Edwin

After he was baptised, King Edwin worked with Paulinus to spread Christianity throughout his own kingdom and beyond. Among those who became Christian under their influence was Readwald, but his majesty's conversion was not exactly thoroughgoing. Although he consented to be baptised, he failed to remove the pagan idols from his palace. Bede the partial and prejudiced historian regarded Readwald's 'syncretism' as a terrible mistake and a betrayal of his new faith.

The King of the East Angles was not the only one to hang on to elements of the old pagan culture after his baptism. The Franks Casket, a chest fashioned from bone, probably in Northumbria around the time Readwald was crowned, was carved with an image of the Adoration of the Magi, but also with scenes from the pagan mythology of the Romans, and ancient Germanic legends.

The continued fascination of the English for tales that had little or nothing to do with Christianity was a source of concern for the English Scholar Alcuin of York. Around 800

CE he wrote from the Continent to an English Bishop called Speratus, protesting not only that he and his followers were eating and drinking too much, but also listening to harpists singing pagan tales during dinner. Referring to a well-known hero who appears fleetingly in the poem Beowulf, Alcuin asked pointedly, 'What has Ingeld to do with Christ?'

The death of Readwald some time in the 620s put Hilda's great-uncle Edwin at the height of his power: now the Northumbrian king was free to become the dominant ruler over much of what we now call England.

Of course not everyone was happy to be dominated in this way, and a Welsh king called Cadwallon ap Cadfan teamed up with Penda, the pagan King of Mercia in the English midlands, to make war on Edwin. In a battle in what was then marsh-country between modern Yorkshire and Lincolnshire – a place called Hatfield Chase – the Northumbrian king and most of his army were killed, on the twelfth of October 633. He had reigned for seventeen years, been a Christian for six of them, and died at the age of forty-eight. His head was recovered and cherished at the unfinished church he had begun at York.

With Edwin gone, Penda and Cadwallon were free to rampage through Northumbria, torturing and killing many of Edwin's subjects, including women and children. Bede tells us that it did not bother the Welsh king that he was killing fellow-Christians, 'it being to this day the custom of the Britons to despise the faith and religion of the English'. Paulinus and Edwin's queen fled from all this mayhem back to the Christian kingdom of Kent, where he was made Bishop of Rochester.

The differences between the Latin Christianity of the English and the Celtic Christianity of the Britons were to have a profound effect on the future life of Hilda. With the death of Edwin and the chaos that followed it, his kingdom of Northumbria reverted to paganism, and was ruled for a time by Cadwallon. The man who united Northumbria again, restoring both order and Christianity, was the future King Oswald of Northumbria, who defeated Cadwallon in either 633 or 634 at the battle of Heavenfield near Hexham in Northumberland. After the battle, the Welsh king was hunted down and killed.

Oswald was not a son of Edwin, but of Edwin's enemy Aethelfrith, the King of Northumbria who had tried to bribe and bully Readwald into killing the young prince. Oswald was a Christian, but not of the same kind as Edwin or Paulinus. Like Edwin during the reign of Aethelfrith, Oswald had spent years in exile, in his case in Dál Riata, a kingdom that encompassed both the west of Scotland and the north-east of the island of Ireland. Here Oswald had learned about and been baptised into the Celtic version of Christianity. When he had secured his position as the new King of Northumbria, he called on the abbey of the island of Iona to send a missionary to convert, or re-convert, his northern Saxons to the faith he had embraced in exile.

The first bishop who was sent made little headway. Oswald's followers would not listen to him, and he returned home with stories of their stubbornness and barbarity. One can imagine the poor prelate, who probably did not speak a word of Anglo-Saxon, trying to explain the Trinity to a bunch of half-drunk warriors, perhaps in the great hall of Oswald's royal castle at Bamburgh on the North Sea coast.

At a *post mortem* meeting on Iona, a monk piped up and suggested that the frustrated bishop had failed because he had led with the more difficult Christian doctrines, whereas he should have offered his listeners 'the milk of more easy doctrine, till, being by degrees nourished with the Word of God, they should be capable of receiving that which is more perfect and of performing the higher precepts of God'. The monk who had compared missionary work to the familiar business of weaning babies onto solid food was called Aidan. Now he was sent to Oswald's kingdom, and met with much more success.

Hilda would have been around twenty when Oswald beat Cadwallon, became the new king of a united Northumbria, and invited missionaries from Iona to convert his people. We know that she had been baptised, along with her great-uncle King Edwin and many others, by Paulinus at York when she was perhaps thirteen, but Bede offers us no direct information about where she was or what she was doing for a full twenty years after that, until she took the veil and became a nun at the age of thirty-three, around the year 647. It is likely that Bede himself had no information about Hilda's life during this time: he dismisses the matter by saying that she lived a secular life up to the age of thirty-three.

If Bede did have information about Hilda's missing years then he might have deliberately left it out of his *Ecclesiastical History* because he meant to write an *ecclesiastical* history, and Hilda had little or nothing to do with ecclesiastical matters at this time. He must also have been conscious of the fact that his history was going to cover events spanning some eight hundred years, and that if he included every detail, his book would become too long. Part of the appeal of the *History* to modern readers is that, even with the inevitable introductions and notes, in English translation it makes a chunky but still manageable single volume.

Authors tackling Hilda's biography tend to gloss over the period from the death of Edwin to c. 647, or assume that the saint was one of those who fled to Kent with Paulinus when Cadwallon in particular was spreading mayhem throughout Edwin's kingdom. Bede does not list Hilda, her mother or her sister among those Paulinus took with him: perhaps they made their own way to Kent, where they spent some of their time trying to make out what was happening elsewhere in Britain. It seems that Hilda herself may have returned to the north before 647, perhaps tempted by the re-Christianisation of Northumbria by Oswald and Aidan. Hilda also spent some time in the kingdom of the East Angles – her older sister Hereswith had married an East Anglian prince around the year 627.

Hilda is identified as a virgin in the Old English Martyrology and in a 1903 book called *Virgin Saints of the Benedictine Order*. It is, however, quite possible that she was married and widowed during the thirty-three years of her life that she lived before taking the veil. Bede does not mention marriage (or any children) as an element of her secular years, but he does not mention that she was a virgin either. A novelist trying to build a coherent story around Hilda might be tempted to have her betrothed at an early age (as was the custom) to some rugged warrior who had spotted her by the light of the roaring fire in Edwin's royal hall; a warrior who then fell with Edwin at Hatfield Chase, leaving Hilda both a widow and a refugee. Since she was nobly-born, Hilda's hypothetical marriage may have not had anything to do with attraction, though. Well-born young ladies were often given in marriage as part of a diplomatic deal between kingdoms.

Despite a strong and promising start, King Oswald did not reign over Edwin's old kingdom for long. Penda and his Welsh allies still stood out against him, and Aidan's patron perished at the Battle of Maserfelth in 641 or 642. The clash may have taken place far from Oswald's Northumbrian home, at Oswestry in Shropshire. As if to show the brutality of the time, the body of the Northumbrian king was dismembered and parts of it hung up on stakes, perhaps as an offering to the pagan gods.

A novelist might have Hilda's hypothetical husband dying with Oswald at this battle, which would 'explain' why Hilda did not choose the cloister soon after Edwin perished. An author with a taste for melodrama might have the aristocratic widow watching helplessly as her hypothetical children by her hypothetical husband were massacred by pagan raiders loyal to Penda, or carried off by some deadly illness.

It is possible, of course, that Hilda managed to remain single until the age of thirty-three, when she became a nun. There are examples of female saints who insisted on remaining virgins though marriages were pressed on them, although it is hard to explain why this version of Hilda, who presumably decided to remain celibate in her teens, waited perhaps fifteen years before she committed herself to the cloister. Saint Bega, whom Hilda may have known, is supposed to have been a beautiful Irish princess who fled to England and became a nun to avoid an arranged marriage.

Margaret of Antioch, the aforementioned fourth-century saint who killed a dragon by giving it an explosive case of indigestion, was introduced to her dragon as a form of torture, as she had displeased the local Roman authorities by refusing to marry one of their high-ranking officials because she wished to remain a virgin. St Anatolia, who tamed the snake that was introduced into her prison-cell, had been imprisoned in the first place because she had refused to marry a pagan. Both therefore died virgins.

There were, of course, married saints who refused to have sex: a saint who appears in Bede's *History* who married due to family pressure but remained celibate was Ethelthryth, wife of King Ecgfrid, the latter being a son of King Oswiu of Northumbria. Bede believed that the chaste Ethelthryth, who was both a younger contemporary and a relative of Hilda, must have remained a virgin despite her marriage, because after her death her body remained incorrupt. Whereas some great ladies, including queens, waited until they were widows before that became nuns, Ethelthryth managed to become a holy sister while her royal husband was still alive.

A year after Oswald was cut up and exposed on the battlefield of Maserfelth, his brother Oswiu arrived with an army to recover what was left of the old king. It is thought that Oswald's head now shares a coffin under the flagstones of Durham Cathedral, with St Cuthbert. Cuthbert is often depicted, in paintings and statues, holding Oswald's head. Oswiu became King of Bernicia, the northern part of Northumbria, in 642, but struggled to rule Deira as well, as his older brother had done. His kingdom was repeatedly attacked by Penda, while his cousin Oswine ruled Deira and Aidan remained bishop of both kingdoms.

Threatened by Oswiu, Oswine went into hiding, as Edwin, Oswald, Oswiu and Hilda's father Hereric had all been forced to do, as a succession of warlike leaders struggled for control of the Anglo-Saxon kingdoms, often resorting to wiping out their own close relatives. Oswine met a fate similar to that faced by Hereric, and narrowly avoided by Edwin – killed by the hosts who had sheltered him, in their home at Gilling, North Yorkshire, in 651.

Oswiu's nephew Oethelwald became king of Deira, but he also became an ally of Penda and the pair teamed up to attack Oswiu. Things came to a head at a battle by the River Winwaed in the winter of 655. This may have been near Leeds. Despite overwhelming odds, Oswiu won, and killed Penda by decapitating him. Part of the Bernician king's success could be attributed to the fact that his nephew Oethelwald's troops changed sides, but Oswiu himself may have remembered that he had pledged twelve of his estates to the church, to be given over in the event of his victory. He had also promised to put his tiny daughter Aelfflaed into a monastery. It may have been on one of the twelve estates Oswiu had gifted to the church that the abbey of Hartlepool was built. By the time little Aelfflaed was old enough to leave home and become a nun at Hartlepool, Hilda was abbess there.

There is a suggestion in some of the sources that the twelve pieces of land Oswiu gave to the church were embarrassingly small. In the chapter on Hilda in her book *The Private Lives of the Saints*, Janina Ramirez suggests that such gifts of land, however extensive they were, were in any case not totally lost to the giver. Oswiu might still have benefited from control of the land, and received some revenues from it. By ensuring that a relative became abbess, such land could also stay in the family, whereas if it was given to a daughter who then married, it would come under her husband's control. Oswiu may have given his daughter Aelfflaed to the church because he knew that, as a princess, she would surely become an abbess, if she lived long enough.

At this distance in time, it is often difficult to line up the dates found in various sources into a convincing sequence. Although the abbey at Hartlepool could hardly have been founded on land given by King Oswiu after the Battle of the Winwaed before the battle took place in 655, sources such as Cuthbert Sharp's 1851 history of Hartlepool suggest that the town's abbey was founded as early as 640, by a nun called Hieu. Sharp also cites earlier sources that suggest that Hieu and the aforementioned Irish princess St Bega may have been one and the same person. Having fled her native Ireland to avoid marriage, she ended up in Northumbria where, during the reign of King Oswald, Aidan instructed her to found the abbey of Hartlepool. According to a thirteenth-century account of her life, Bega performed many miracles, some of them long after her death. At some point in the twelfth century she is supposed to have settled a dispute about the extent of her monastery's lands by causing snow to fall all around it – but none fell on the monastery's lands.

It is likely that the thirteenth-century author of the Life of Bega confused Abbess Hieu with a nun called Begu, mentioned by Bede, whom we will meet later. He may also have got the name 'Bega' not from a person at all but from an arm-ring kept at the monastery of St Bees in Cumbria, that was supposed to perform miracles. The Anglo-Saxon word for a ring or bracelet was 'beag': perhaps some careless scribe had mixed up the 'a' and the 'g' to make 'bega'.

Hilda from the book *Virgin Saints of the Benedictine Order.*

Hilda the Nun

Although Hilda eventually ended up as abbess of Hartlepool, she spent at least two years as a nun elsewhere before she came to the place Bede calls Hereteu. First she went to the kingdom of the East Angles, which her sister Hereswith, now a widow, had left to cross over into France to live as a nun there. Hilda's plan was to join her sister. Bede tells us that the then King of the East Angles was an ally of Hilda's. This would have been King Anna, a nephew of Readwald. Bede praises this monarch for his piety: as many as five of his children may have become saints. In much the same way that his uncle Readwald had sheltered Edwin, Anna protected the exiled King Cenwalh of Wessex. Anna convinced Cenwalh to become a Christian, and stood as his god-father at his baptism. When he regained his kingdom, Cenwalh set about returning Wessex to the Christian fold.

Despite his saintly family and infectious enthusiasm for Christianity, King Anna was still by necessity a warrior-king. He and his saintly son Jurmin were killed in battle against Penda, King of the Mercians, at Bulcamp in Suffolk in 654.

Although Bede for one gives us no reason to doubt that Hilda was remarkably pious, and longed for the life of the cloister, there may have been reasons beyond simple faith that caused her to choose the religious way of life. By the time she made her decision to take the veil, Hilda may have been a widow in her early thirties, without surviving children. She had royal connections to various parts of England, but life as a sort of court hanger-on, which may have been how she and her mother and sister had lived under King Edwin, may have had limited appeal.

Re-marriage and (more?) children may have been a prospect, but then she would have lost a great deal of control over her own life, and ended up in an inferior position, perhaps under some crass warrior-thegn. Living through some of the violent times she had seen, Hilda may have longed for a life somewhat removed from that of the petty warrior-kings and their endless wars. If she had become a dependant of her ally King Anna, he may have felt entitled to marry her off into some other royal family, as part of a diplomatic deal. Throughout the middle ages, women fled into abbeys to avoid this kind of marriage.

An example of a widowed queen who became a nun rather than re-marry was the wife of King Edwin. As Ramirez suggests in her *Private Lives of the Saints*, Ethelburg may have opted for the holy life so as to avoid being re-married on the orders of her brother Eadbald. Although Hilda was not so high on the social scale as Queen Ethelburg, their two cases may have been similar, and Ramirez suggests that Hilda may have known Ethelburg as a widow living in Kent, and been inspired by her example. Ethelburg went on to found an abbey at Lyminge.

In order to live, in effect, as a nun somewhere in Anna's kingdom, Hilda may have felt that she needed the approval and support of a prominent local churchman; perhaps a bishop. If Hilda first began to live the cloistered life in East Anglia after 647, then the relevant prelate would have been Thomas, Bishop of Dunwich, whom Bede tells us originally came from the fen country around Ely, home to the tribe of the Gyrwas. At this time, Dunwich, on the North Sea coast of Suffolk, must have been large and impressive enough to be worthy to be the headquarters of a bishop, but in the more than thirteen hundred years since Hilda's time the sea itself has eroded away so much of the town that it is now a mere coastal village. This is the place of which it is said that sometimes the bells of the drowned churches can be heard clanging under the sea.

Like much else in Bede's great history, Hilda's year-long stay in East Anglia is not fully explained. Once she had decided to be a nun in France, why did she hesitate to cross the English Channel and join her sister? Can it be that she enjoyed being in authority over her tiny cell of like-minded devotees, and shrank from the prospect of being placed under a harsh monastic Rule that was not of her own devising, and having to obey an abbess? Or was she enjoying living with the like-minded Queen Ethelburg?

It is possible that Hilda did not, like Gregory the Great, organise her own community around herself during her year of waiting in East Anglia. She may have lived alone as a kind of hermit or anchorite, or together with others in an established monastery under someone else's authority. A possible candidate would be the abbey at Soham in Cambridgeshire, founded by Felix of Burgundy, the first bishop of the East Angles, and Bishop Thomas's immediate predecessor. Bede, our main source on Hilda, does not, however, mention where the saint stayed in East Anglia, or why or who with. It may be that as the sister of Hereswith, and perhaps the widow of some very important but unidentified East Anglian nobleman, Hilda was able to attach herself to the court of her ally King Anna, but without being identified by him as a dependent whom he could marry off.

Many sources suggest that the French abbey that Hereswith went to, and where her sister Hilda longed to join her, was at Chelles to the east of Paris; but here again we have problems lining up the dates. Chelles Abbey was not founded until at least 657, and perhaps as late as 660, by Balthild, the saintly wife of the Frankish King Clovis II. Like Hereswith, Balthild was an Anglo-Saxon living in the kingdom of the Franks, but unlike Hilda's sister, Clovis's queen had been forced to go there as a slave. Like the beautiful Anglian boys who had caught Gregory's eye in the slave market at Rome, Balthild's looks got her noticed, so that she rose from slave to queen consort.

In his DNB article on Hilda, Alan Thacker suggests that Hereswith may actually have gone to the abbey at Jouarre, or the one at Faremoutiers, both of which are also east of Paris, and both of which were founded earlier than Chelles, which was a sister-house of Jouarre. As an Anglo-Saxon aristocrat who had married into the royal family of the East Angles, Hereswith might have felt particularly welcome at

Faremoutiers, where she may have lived long enough to see two royal East Anglian sisters become abbess, one after the other. These were Saethryth, a step-daughter of Hilda's ally King Anna of East Anglia, and Aethelburh, one of his saintly daughters.

As well as meeting (or renewing her friendship with) some noble Anglo-Saxon ladies at Faremoutiers, Hereswith would have encountered a Celtic variety of Christianity similar to that which had been introduced into Northumbria by Oswald and Aidan. The reason why that form of Christianity was present in Continental Europe was partly because of the efforts of a remarkable Irish saint, monk and missionary called St Columbanus (who should not be confused with St Columba, a slightly earlier figure).

According to a biography of Columbanus written by one Jonas, who became a monk at Bobbio, an Italian monastery the Irishman had founded, Columbanus's mother had dreamed about her child in a way very similar to Hilda's mother. Shortly after his conception, the saints's mother dreamed not of a gleaming necklace, but of the sun itself rising out of her body. Her child became a monk in Ireland, then in 590, when he was nearing fifty, he was given permission to go abroad as a missionary, with twelve companions.

They found Christianity in a sorry state in what we now call France, and set about establishing schools and monasteries. The later abbeys at Jouarre, Chelles and Faremoutiers were not directly founded by them, but the founder of Jouarre had been inspired by a visit of Columbanus; the founder of Faremoutiers had also encountered the Irishman, and the abbey at Chelles followed the Rule of Columbanus, a set of laws devised by the saint for the running of a monastery.

Columbanus's Rule was extremely strict, demanding obedience even 'to the point of death', which would seem to suggest that an abbot or abbess had the right to order a monk or nun to do something that would put their own life in danger. A bland, meagre vegetarian diet was insisted on in the Rule, as was silence, hard work, fasting, prayer, poverty and what we would now call sleep deprivation. Let the monk 'come to bed exhausted and fall asleep on his feet', the saint commanded, and added, 'he must be forced to rise before sleep has been completed'.

Although, if she had ever gone to live in France, Hilda would have encountered a Celtic form of Christianity that may have been familiar to her, the mere possibility of such a move is a reminder that Christianity at this time was a truly international phenomenon. Churchmen spoke and wrote a form of Latin that was understood by their counterparts across a wide swath of Europe and beyond. The monasteries that were such an essential part of the structure of the Church in many areas were, some of them, store-houses of the wisdom of the ages, in the form of manuscript copies of ancient classics from a range of traditions.

Like Augustine of Canterbury, Paulinus and Aidan, Columbanus and his followers were monks who relied on local rulers to help them with their work of Christianising or re-Christianising parts of Europe. Their approach, and their status as monks, necessarily had an effect on how the Christianity they preached developed. It is possible that the

Latin Christianity King Edwin had established in Northumbria with the help of Paulinus was easily wiped out because once the monks and aristocrats who had promoted it had fled or gone into hiding there was no healthy grass-roots Christianity among ordinary people to keep it going. If the life of a monk or nun was seen as the ultimate in Christian perfection, then surely there was a danger that the most devoted people in all classes would disappear from everyday life into the isolation of the cloister, sometimes in another country. If pious folk donned the monastic habit in early life, then their vow of celibacy meant that they could not pass on their faith to any children of their own.

The missionaries' reliance on local rulers was surely connected to the tendency of the ruling class to dominate monastic communities: the class system of the secular world was mirrored in the hierarchy of the abbeys and the priesthood. Since only the secular rulers had the land, money and power to cause churches and religious houses to be built, they expected members of their own families to be put in charge of such institutions.

Whether Hilda's prominence in the religious sphere was due to her royal blood or her innate personal qualities is unclear: she probably succeeded because she possessed both. In any case, Aidan thought that she was so essential to the continued success of Christianity in Northumbria that he contacted Hilda in East Anglia and begged her to abandon her dream of joining her sister in a French abbey. She was needed in the north.

At first Hilda lived in a small monastic community on the north bank of the River Wear, together with a few companions. If she had not lived alone as a nun during her year among the East Angles, it seems reasonable to suppose that some or all of her associates in East Anglia joined her by the great river that tuns through both Durham and Sunderland. Exactly where this small community was on the north bank of the Wear is not known. Bede tells us that the land given to Hilda for this small 'cell' was sufficient to support one peasant family, an acreage known to the Anglo-Saxons as a 'hide', from an old word for a family.

Although Hilda's mysterious Wearside cell cannot have been very big, many of the monastic communities celebrated by Bede in his *History* would have been modest by the standards of the later medieval period. The fact that, like many Anglo-Saxon settlements at the time, they would have been made up of plain wooden houses might mean that they were sometimes hard to tell apart from secular villages and hamlets. An advantage of such buildings was that they were made from the plentiful wood that grew in the forests round about and, if they burned down, as they were liable to do, they could easily be evacuated and re-built. Later builders of churches and monasteries brought stone and stone-masons from distant places, as the Romans had done: one suspects that the barn-like early structures of the Anglo-Saxons required very few specialist skills to put up, refurbish or repair.

There is a striking account of the dangerously inflammable nature of these buildings in the *Ecclesiastical History*. Bede tells us that St Aidan died leaning against the wooden buttress of a church, and when Penda burned down the same church during one of his raids, the buttress was found to be intact. It was re-used in the new church that was built on the site, and when that was burned down by accident, the buttress was still unburned, 'though the fire broke through the very holes of the nails wherewith it was fixed to the building'.

One drawback of such buildings is that their remains are hard for archaeologists to detect. If all the wood has rotted away and the plaster crumbled to dust, what might remain are only post-holes, where the bottoms of the uprights were buried, and perhaps piles of stones heaped around them to keep them upright.

If well-built, these stone-free buildings could be cool in summer and warm in winter, unlike stone-build castles, churches and other buildings, some of which are cold all year round. Although to modern eyes they may seem fragile and temporary, they were evidently able to stand up to some horrendous weather. Hilda's later abbey at Hartlepool, which comprised a cluster of such buildings, stood on an exposed headland with the raging North Sea on three sides.

It may be that Aidan begged Hilda to return to the north because he thought she had a valuable contribution to make to the life of the Church in Northumbria. It may be that he placed her in charge of her modest riverside cell to check that she really had the leadership qualities he thought he saw in her. Here, also, she may have been less tempted to decide to join her sister in France. Given what happened a year after Hilda returned to the north, Aidan may have been keeping Hilda in reserve until he could find a way to put her in charge of the abbey at Hartlepool, as a successor to Abbess Hieu.

Hilda the Abbess

Hieu, the Irishwoman who was said to be the first woman in Northumbria to become a nun, let alone an abbess and the foundress of an abbey, seems to have been in charge of the abbey at Hartlepool, an abbey she had founded, for a very short time before she left and was replaced by Hilda. Hieu spent her remaining years at the second abbey she founded, at Healaugh near Tadcaster in Yorkshire. It is possible that the names of both Hartlepool and Healaugh were inspired by Hieu's name, though the charming idea that Hartlepool was named as a place where deer came to drink has many supporters.

The founding abbess of Hartlepool may have been persuaded to leave because under her authority the place was deemed to be not quite up to scratch. It may be that she had had good intentions, but had struggled to impose her authority because, as an Irishwoman, the Anglo-Saxon brothers and sisters in her abbey had identified her with the Celts whom their ancestors had been fighting for centuries. We may also be able to attribute some of Hilda's success to the fact that she was from a noble local family, and would have commanded respect even if she had never become a nun or an abbess. It may be that Aidan's royal collaborator King Oswiu wanted her in charge of Hartlepool because she was a relative, and he hoped to be able to control the abbey and its lands through her.

Hilda set about bringing or restoring order to the abbey at Hartlepool, establishing a proper monastic Rule. Whether this was the Rule of Columbanus which would have been followed in the monastery where Hilda's sister lived over in France, or Benedict's Rule, or something else is not known. What is known is that at her new wind-swept home Hilda was regularly visited by Aidan and other learned people, whom Bede says loved and admired her, and were happy to give advice and guidance.

As well as taking on a perhaps troubled abbey, Hilda now also had the responsibility of looking after Aelfflaed, the tiny princess King Oswiu had promised to devote to the religious life, if God granted him victory against Penda in the Battle of the Winwaed. The skeletons of men, women and children have been found in the monastic burial-grounds uncovered at Hartlepool, but Aelfflaed did not die there as a child. She lived to be as old as sixty, and died in 714 not at Hartlepool but at the abbey Hilda may have founded at Whitby. Aelfflaed probably transferred from Hartlepool to Whitby when Hilda went there.

The practice of dedicating children to the church at an age when they are too young to make intelligent decisions about their futures resembles the medieval habit of betrothing aristocratic children to their equivalents in other kingdoms, as part of a diplomatic deal, long before modern people would consider them old enough to think about marriage. There is a sense in which those children 'farmed out' to alien courts were gifts, peace-offerings or even hostages, and bearing in mind that Hilda would have assembled a kind of monastic court around herself at Hartlepool, and that nuns were considered to have married Jesus, Oswiu's gift of his daughter to the Church does look like one of those dynastic deals.

Like a foreign princess newly-arrived as a bride in some strange palace, Aelfflaed would no doubt have received special treatment at Hartlepool and then Whitby. As a nobly-born girl, she would probably have felt very much at home, because these monasteries housed quite a number of high-born ladies who had chosen life in the cloister.

Unlike many of the kings of this time, Aelfflaed's father did not die in battle. Instead he died with his boots off in 670, at the age of fifty-eight, and was perhaps buried at Hilda's abbey at Whitby. His wife Eanfled, Aelfflaed's mother, became a nun herself soon after she became a widow, and when Hilda died in 680 mother and daughter became joint abbesses.

While Hilda was still alive, Aelfflaed might have felt that she had two mothers to hand – her biological mother, and the abbess who had in effect fostered her since before she could remember. Since Hilda was also a relative (they shared a great-grandfather; King Aelle of Deira) Aelfflaed might have regarded Hilda as a very learned and distinguished aunt, though Bede tells us that everybody loved Hilda so much that they called her 'mother'.

When Hilda died, Aelfflaed would have been under thirty, and it may be that she could not at first become sole abbess because she was just too young. If, as is possible, Whitby Abbey also had a sister-house at Strensall in Yorkshire or elsewhere, it may be that Aelfflaed stayed at one place, and her mother Eanfled at another. As she grew into her role and became sole abbess, Aelfflaed became surprisingly influential, in both the religious and political spheres. The fact that her father had been a king, and that her brother Ecgfrith became King of Northumbria in 670, must have helped.

In 684 Aelfflaed consulted St Cuthbert about her brother's plans to make him a bishop. As well as later consenting to be a bishop, once Ecgrith had condescended to visit him to beg him to do so, Cuthbert was a monk, hermit, priest, missionary and miracle-worker. Perhaps the most loveable of our Northern Saints, Cuthbert lies under the flagstones of the feretory in Durham Cathedral, and could be said to be the whole reason the cathedral, and even the city itself is there today. Bede, who sleeps at the other end of the great church, not only included Cuthbert in his *History*, but also wrote both prose and verse biographies of him. Born around 634, Cuthbert was an older contemporary of both Hilda and Aelfflaed.

Around 685 Trumwine, a refugee bishop, came to live at Aelfflaed's abbey. He had been chosen to be bishop over the Picts in what we now call Scotland, who were supposed to be under the control of Aelfflaed's brother, King Ecgrith of Northumbria. Ecgrith's punitive military expedition against these rebellious northerners went badly wrong and he was killed at the Battle of Nechtansmere in 685. The disaster was what made poor Bishop Trumwine a refugee. Trumwine was a friend of Cuthbert, who was still alive when the bishop fled to Whitby: he was able to supply Bede with a story about Cuthbert's childhood, which the chronicler included in his prose life of the saint.

The presence of Trumwine at Whitby shows how one habit of the secular rulers of the time, that of protecting important refugees from other kingdoms, was carried on by members of the ruling class who found themselves in charge in religious contexts. The bishop's presence must have added greatly to the prestige of the abbey, as did Aelfflaed's determination to retrieve the bones of her grandfather King Edwin from the battlefield at Hatfield Chase and have them re-buried there.

We may ask how his majesty's bones were found after so many years. It seems that a priest called Trimma was visited in a dream, by a mysterious man who told him to go to the site of Edwin's last battle, recover the royal bones and take them to Aelfflaed and Eanfled. A Lincolnshire man called Teoful knew where the bones were, added Trimma's dream-visitor. At first Trimma ignored the man of his dreams, but when he came a third time the priest set off, found Teoful and, at the second attempt, successfully exhumed Edwin.

Trimma's tale is told in the aforementioned Life of Gregory the Great written by an anonymous monk of Whitby, which was produced while Aelfflaed was abbess there. The production of the book itself added to the prestige of Hilda's foundation, and reminded readers of the links between Aelfflaed and the great Gregory. Her grandfather was baptised by Paulinus, who had been sent by the celebrated pope. The book also focused on Gregory's mission to the English, although the north of England had been re-converted, during Hilda's life-time, by an Irish monk. There is no mention of Aidan in the Whitby Life of Gregory.

Hieu's abbey at Hartlepool, where Hilda came to live with her ward the future Abbess Aelfflaed of Whitby, may have comprised the first permanent settlement in the town, or perhaps the first for many years. It may have been spread across much of the southern end of the town's Headland, a fist-shaped limestone peninsular that sticks out into the sea, pointing roughly east-south-east. In Hieu's time the water to the west of the Headland would have formed a natural harbour, sheltered from the worst of the wind and waves, which has now been improved by much building out into the water. Here visitors to the abbey could have landed in their ships, and goods that were best not brought overland could also be unloaded. The buildings must have included at least one church, and there is archaeological evidence for numerous small buildings where the monks and nuns of this so called 'double monastery' could have lived alone, or in pairs.

The abbey which Hilda took over may have been concentrated around the site of the current Parish Church of St Hilda, parts of which date from Norman times. This is on the western side of the headland, convenient for the old landing-place. On display in the church is one of the Saxon name-stones discovered by workmen digging foundations for new houses in the town in 1833. These had been found near the bodies in a monastic grave-yard. The example on display in the church is a thick limestone slab just under a foot square, inscribed with a cross, the Greek letters Alpha and Omega and the name Hildthryth written in the runic alphabet that the Anglo-Saxons brought with them from their Germanic homelands.

Alpha and Omega are the first and last letters of the Greek alphabet: they are important for Christians because in the New Testament Book of Revelation it is revealed that Jesus is 'the Alpha and the Omega, the First and the Last, the Beginning and the End' (Revelation 22:13). With the cross, the fish and various other symbols, the Greek letters have remained part of Christian imagery.

Quite a stir was caused by the discovery of these stones back in 1833. A long article appeared in the *Durham Advertiser* newspaper, and an anonymous letter was printed in *The Gentleman's Magazine*. The well-informed author of the letter commented on the excellent condition of the stone that still remains at Hartlepool: 'the chiselling . . . is as crisp and sharp as if it had been cut yesterday, and the letters are smooth and well-finished'. One of the workmen who discovered the 1833 stones was evidently so impressed by what collectors were prepared to pay for such things that when he later found himself living in Bedfordshire he deliberately created a new one, which he 'found' in a railway cutting. This he sold to a local lady, who donated it to the Bedford museum.

The Bedfordshire fraud is reminiscent of an episode in Charles Dickens's first novel *The Posthumous Papers of the Pickwick Club* (or *Pickwick Papers*) which began to appear as a serial just three years after the discovery of the first Saxon name-stones at Hartlepool. In Chapter XI, Mr Pickwick spots an unusual stone in the garden of a man called Bill Stumps, who lives at Cobham in Surrey. Engraved on the surface of the stone is the baffling inscription:

+

B I L S T

U M

P S H I

S. M.

A R K

Believing it to be of historical importance, Pickwick buys the stone from Stumps and proceeds to write 'a pamphlet, containing ninety-six pages of very small print, and twenty-seven different readings of the inscription'. The furore that greets the discovery of the stone leads to such bitter controversy 'that three old gentlemen cut off their eldest sons with a shilling a-piece for presuming to doubt the antiquity of the fragment—and that one enthusiastic individual cut himself off prematurely, in despair at being unable to fathom its meaning'. Eventually a Mr Blotton establishes that the stone was inscribed by the Cobham man who sold it to Pickwick for ten shillings (worth about forty pounds in today's money). Untangled, the inscription reads '+ BILL STUMPS HIS MARK'.

A stone similar to the Hildryth stone, and more burials, were discovered at Hartlepool in 1838, and it is likely that these unusual grave-goods belonged with the skeletons of nuns and monks from the monastery founded by Hieu. It is unclear exactly why these so-called name-stones were made or how they were used. The startled nineteenth-century workmen who first came across them claimed that the skulls of many of the skeletons they found were resting on stones, but whether large stones like the Hildryth stone were used like pillows in this way is uncertain.

In a chapter in a 1999 book called *Northumbria's Golden Age* Elisabeth Okasha suggests that the larger name-stones may have been placed on the surface above the burials like modern grave-stones. Okasha suggests that the reason why some of them are in such good condition is because they very quickly sank into the ground or were covered with soil, which protected them.

More artefacts relating to the monastery at Hartlepool were uncovered in the twentieth century: in 1984 evidence of high-quality metal-working was found, including a beautiful little clay mould of a calf (symbol of St Luke) blowing a trumpet. This would have been used to make a small rectangular metal medallion.

From 1994 British TV viewers have been educated and entertained by a series called *Time Team*, originally presented by the acclaimed actor Tony Robinson. In the series, a team of experts, including archaeologists, spend a few days in a place where they expect to find archaeological remains just waiting to be dug up. In 1999 the team descended on Hartlepool: though they were plagued by rain, cold and mist, they managed to make holes in various locations on the Headland, including the Town Moor, a traffic island and the car-park of the local Conservative Party HQ.

Their main finds were the post-holes of typical Anglo-Saxon buildings, the diminutive skeleton of a nun (found in a private garden) and a small part of the metal clasp mechanism of a book of the type designed to be hooked shut like a farm-gate. As well as excavating, the team recreated a typical hand-made book of the time, with a metal medallion based on the calf mould found in 1984 used as a cover decoration.

Beyond these finds from the nineteenth and twentieth centuries there seems to be little archaeological data to add to our knowledge about the abbey at Hartlepool. The seventeenth-century Durham writer Robert Hegge mentions the destruction of the abbey in the year 800 in his book *The Legend of St Cuthbert* – if this happened, it may have been Viking raiders who were responsible, but over the years archaeologists have found no evidence of wilful destruction here. It may be that the abbey simply went into a decline, despite Hilda's best efforts to reform it and set it on a sustainable path.

Namestone from Hartlepool.

Whitby

Bede tells us that after several years at Hartlepool Hilda proceeded to set up a new abbey (or perhaps bring order to an old one) at a place called Streanaeshalch. By this time Aidan, who died in 651, was no longer in the picture: perhaps he looked down from heaven and noted with satisfaction that his protégé was growing into her role very nicely. She had perhaps started the sanctified part of her life in East Anglia, either in a monastery, or as a hermit, or with a small group of like-minded friends. Then she had set up her own small cell on the Wear, then taken control of what might have been a troubled foundation at Hartlepool. Now she was perhaps setting up a new abbey that would grow to become a very significant place.

'Streanaeshalch' has long been assumed to be Whitby, but a chapter in a 2003 book called *The Cross Goes North* suggested that the place Bede had in mind may not have been Whitby at all, but somewhere else entirely. In their chapter, 'The Confusion of Conversion: Streanaeshalch, Strensall and Whitby and the Northumbrian Church' the authors suggest another Yorkshire settlement, the village of Strensall, just north of York and over forty miles from Whitby. No remains of an Anglo-Saxon abbey have been found at Strensall, but a web-page that forms part of the York Historic Environment Record suggests that the remains of a moat visible there may have had something to do with the hypothetical abbey. The building that now stands by the moat is a much-altered seventeenth-century farmhouse.

Alan Thacker, author of the 2004 Dictionary of National Biography article on Hilda, gives space to the Strensall idea, and also airs the possibility that Whitby and Strensall were two parts of the same abbey, located some forty miles apart. This arrangement is reminiscent of Jarrow/Monkwearmouth, two monasteries in one, which was the home of Bede, our chronicler. Jarrow and Monkwearmouth are, however, only seven miles apart. If Bede's Streanaeshalch was not Whitby but Strensall, then the famous Synod of Whitby, of which more later, may in fact have been the Synod of Strensall.

Since no remains of an Anglo-Saxon monastery have ever been found at Strensall, but plenty have been uncovered at Whitby, I have written the relevant parts of this book as if Bede's Streanaeshalch were indeed Whitby; though it is as well for readers to remember that the two places may not have been the same.

At least three of the monasteries with which Hilda was associated were by the sea or on navigable rivers, if we assume that her mysterious cell on the north bank of the Wear was on a part of that river that could be reached in a boat. Her sea-side monasteries at Hartlepool and Whitby were near good harbours, and if it is true that she set up an abbey at Strensall, then her lost abbey there would have had access to the River Foss, a tributary of the Ouse, which runs through York.

The temptation to build on rivers or by the sea at this time arose from the fact that despite the survival of long stretches of Roman road in the interior, the existence of a network of ancient track-ways, and the tempestuous character of the North Sea, a great deal of movement, both of people and goods, went up and down the east coast.

It helped that the Anglo-Saxons seem to have been good sailors. It is thought that it was their Continental ancestors who invented so-called 'clinker' or 'lap strake' ships and boats, the hulls of which were made from overlapping planks held together with rivets. These were lighter, faster, stronger and more water-tight than the craft they replaced. In the eighties and nineties of the last century scaled-down replicas of Anglo-Saxon ships were made and tried out.

The *Sae Wylfing*, a half-size replica of the Sutton Hoo ship, was launched in 1993. In a chapter in the 1999 book *Northumbria's Golden Age* (edited by Jane Hawkes and Susan Mills) Edwin and Joyce Gifford wrote that the *Sae Wylfing* 'looks, feels and sails like a thoroughbred but handles like a large, docile family dinghy, being stable, easy to steer and predictable'. In Hilda's time, such 'thoroughbreds', unfamiliar to modern sailors, were likely sailed by people who had sailed similar vessels all their lives, whose parents and grand-parents may also have sailed them, and knew all their tricks and the tricks of the waters they sailed on.

As well as agricultural and industrial goods, raw materials and other goods from elsewhere on the coast of Great Britain, settlements with direct or indirect access to the sea could also get hold of more exotic and far-fetched items, since they were connected by water to a network of trade and communication that stretched over thousands of miles through Europe and beyond. Thus in theory letters and gifts could arrive in out-of-the-way places like Strensall, from Rome and even the imperial court at Constantinople in modern-day Turkey.

Abbeys and other settlements on rivers could also benefit from the edible fish that could be found in them, in greater numbers than in many places today, because there was then little or no man-made pollution. Near the sea, it was also easier to supplement one's diet with shellfish. Fish in particular was important for abbey kitchens since on certain days Christians were not supposed to eat meat from birds or mammals.

The golden age of abbeys with access to the sea came to an end in 793, over sixty years after Bede completed his *Ecclesiastical History*, and more than a century after the death of Hilda. It was in that year that the Vikings raided Lindisfarne Priory, destroying the church, making off with many valuables and either killing or enslaving the monks. It was at Lindisfarne, also known as Holy Island, that Bishop Aidan had established the headquarters of his mission, in sight of King Oswald's fort at Bamburgh.

It was also here that Cuthbert was first buried. The body of this much-loved saint was found to be miraculously incorrupt when it was exhumed after the Viking raid.

Guarded by devotees called the Haliwerkfolk, Cuthbert's remains lodged in various places, including the old Roman town of Chester-le-Street, before finding their final resting-place at Durham.

If Hilda's Streanaeshalch was indeed Whitby, it seems that in her part of the seventh century there was little fear that raiders from the sea would attack and loot coastal settlements. In the fourth century CE the Romans had not been so sanguine about the chances for peace along Britain's North Sea coast. It was then that a string of coastal signal stations was constructed, on the orders of a general called Theodosius. In the days before radio or telephones, these stations all had to be visible from the next station in the line, so that messages could be conveyed rapidly over long distances. Many of these stations were in the form of small stone forts.

Since the North Sea stations also had a sea view, they could convey news about potential enemies drawing near across the waves. It is thought that there was one of these stations at Whitby, although its remains may long ago have been claimed by the sea due to coastal erosion (by which time much if not all of its stone would probably have been looted for re-use). Bede suggests that the name 'Streanaeshalch' came from the Latin '*sinus fari*', meaning 'bay of the lighthouse', though whether the Roman signal stations were also used as lighthouses is unclear.

What is clear is that Hilda's new abbey at Streanaeshalch was at least intended as a kind of lighthouse for Christianity in Northumbria: providing light in the darkness, bringing yearning souls into a safe harbour, and helping them to avoid the rocks and shallows of paganism or heresy. Whether or not Hilda founded the monastery at Streanaeshalch, she quickly set about running it in an orderly way, imposing a proper monastic Rule on the brothers and sisters, as she had at Hartlepool. Bede tells us:

> . . . she put this monastery under the same rule of monastic life as the former; and taught there the strict observance of justice, piety, chastity, and other virtues, and particularly of peace and charity; so that, after the example of the primitive Church, no one there was rich, and none poor, for they had all things common, and none had any private property. Her prudence was so great, that not only meaner men in their need, but sometimes even kings and princes, sought and received her counsel; she obliged those who were under her direction to give so much time to reading of the Holy Scriptures, and to exercise themselves so much in works of justice, that many might readily be found there fit for the priesthood and the service of the altar.

Reading Bede's catalogue of Hilda's achievements at Streanaeshalch, it is tempting to imagine what an abbey would have been like without 'the strict observance of justice, piety, chastity, and other virtues'. In a double monastery of men and women, a lack of chastity might have led to love-affairs between the monks and nuns, illegitimate children and much scandal. Shortly after Hilda's time, such a breakdown of discipline was noted at the abbey at Coldingham. There, Bede tells us, none of the monks or nuns were 'busy about the health' of their souls except their abbess, Aebba (a sister of the Northumbrian kings Oswald and Oswiu). The rest:

. . . are either sunk in slothful sleep, or are awake in order to commit sin; for even the cells that were built for prayer or reading, are now converted into places of feasting, drinking, talking, and other delights; the very virgins dedicated to God, laying aside the respect due to their profession, whensoever they are at leisure, apply themselves to weaving fine garments, wherewith to adorn themselves like brides, to the danger of their state, or to gain the friendship of strange men.

It was thought that the result of this laxness was the loss of the abbey (the site of which is now in Berwickshire) to fire. Bede's account of the irregularities at Coldingham, which were discovered by a visiting monk, is interesting because though it begins with an account of a general laziness that may apply to both monks and nuns, it quickly focuses on crimes specific to the sisters.

It is also interesting that it is alleged that those alluring clothes are being put together to attract 'strange men'; which presumably does not mean the monks who were living on the same site. Weaving, together with embroidery and other work with fabrics, was seen as a ladylike occupation, and loom-weights (a typical find in Anglo-Saxon digs) were recovered from Whitby in the last century. If they were not making elaborate clothes as gifts for outsiders, the Streanaeshalch nuns may have been occupied making the fabric for plain habits for themselves, or perhaps fashioning gorgeous altar-cloths and the like for their monastery church or churches.

If it is true that in the abbey at Whitby no one 'was rich, and none poor' because everything was shared, then that was quite remarkable, given that some of the brothers and sisters are known to have come from rich aristocratic families. Bede's reference to 'the primitive Church' calls to mind the practice of the surviving followers of Jesus and the growing ranks of their own followers, as related in the second chapter of the New Testament Book of Acts. Here we learn that:

 . . . all that believed were together, and had all things common; and sold their possessions and goods, and parted them to all men, as every man had need.

(Acts 2, 44-5, KJV)

Later in Acts the story is told of Ananias and Sapphira, who sell some land and put most of the proceeds in the communal pot, but hold back some of the money for themselves. Both die suddenly in the presence of St Peter, because of their dishonesty (Acts 5, 1-10).

Though the people in Hilda's charge at Whitby are supposed to have shared all their wealth, there is no suggestion that the state of their finances was reflected in their status within the hierarchy of the abbey. It is clear that nobly-born monks and nuns, such as Hilda herself, Aebba of Coldingham and Hilda's ward Aelfflaed, could expect to be 'fast-tracked' into senior positions. And there is no suggestion in Bede that Hilda's charges were expected to muck in and do all kinds of work around the abbey and its lands. Manual work was later embraced by the Cistercian monks, but their order was not founded until 1098, over three hundred years after Hilda's death. No, it seems that the farming, cooking, cleaning and other manual jobs were done by servants of the abbey, much as they would have been done around the house and lands of a royal or aristocratic estate.

It is unlikely that many of the abbey's lay servants ever became nuns, monks or priests, despite their proximity to and regular contact with such people. An exception was Caedmon, who seems to have been employed as a cowman at Streanaeshalch, and was 'well advanced in years' when he completed the seventh-century religious equivalent of the journey of a Victorian boot-boy through the green baize door behind which the servants lived, to take up his place with the rest of the grand family at dinner.

The skill which made Hilda regard Caedmon as worthy of this momentous change was his ability to compose verses in the English of the time. The odd thing was that the humble cowman, whose name suggests that he was at least part Celt, actually had no talent for poetry before he was 'well advanced in years'. When the harp was being passed round after dinner in the great hall, and everyone was taking their turn to sing by the fire, Caedmon had a tendency to make himself scarce.

One day as he fled from the hall and the dreaded harp, Caedmon went to sleep in the cow-shed, as it was his turn to sleep there. In a dream, a mysterious stranger visited him and told him to sing. Despite his protests, the stranger persisted, and gave him a large enough subject for his song: creation itself. Caedmon went on to become the poet-monk of Streanaeshalch, and in keeping with his new status, only composed verse on holy subjects, including:

. . . the creation of the world, the origin of man, and all the history of Genesis, the departure of the children of Israel out of Egypt, their entrance into the promised land, and many other histories from Holy Scripture; the Incarnation, Passion, Resurrection of our Lord, and His Ascension into heaven; the coming of the Holy Ghost, and the teaching of the Apostles . . .

Caedmon is called the first English poet, though the Old English or Anglo-Saxon language he used is incomprehensible to most modern English speakers. The tradition of verse in his language continued from his day for nearly four hundred years to the Norman Conquest of 1066, after which Old English went into decline and the ruling class spoke Norman French. Only about thirty thousand lines of Old English poetry survive, including just one short poem from Caedmon. The masterpiece of Anglo-Saxon verse is the epic *Beowulf*, written perhaps three hundred years after Caedmon's time.

Hilda's insistence on the reading of scripture as a fit occupation for monks and nuns is something that demands attention. Such learning presupposes books, but these were extremely rare and precious in Hilda's day. The celebrated Lindisfarne Gospels, produced some forty years after the death of Hilda, reflects not only the culture and artistry of the monks who produced it, but also the Church's willingness to put considerable resources into such a project. The pages of this and other contemporary books produced in the West were made of animal skins: the hides of no fewer than one hundred and fifty calves went into the production of the astonishing Gospels, which are about the size of a very large modern art-book.

That the Church in Northumbria at this time could spare all this valuable leather, which could have gone into shoes, tack for horses, clothes and even armour, says a lot about its control of land, labour, money and other resources. Turning the raw skins into parchment or vellum required time, specialised equipment, dedicated premises and skilled craftsmen. This must have meant that making books from scratch, even if they were not gorgeously decorated and sumptuously bound like the Lindisfarne Gospels, represented an eye-watering outlay of resources. Gifts or loans of books were likewise important events, so that building up even a modest library in a quiet corner of a new abbey was a giddying ambition.

One consequence of the rarity and extreme preciousness of books in the age of Hilda and her successors was that authors like Bede were keen to show off how many books they had actually handled and read. Even volumes that they had only heard of would be mentioned with reverence. Drawing on what must have been an exceptional library at Wearmouth/Jarrow, the author of the *Ecclesiastical History* was by no means bashful about having accessed a wide range of literature, including older British chronicles, scripture, the works of Gregory the Great, and writings by pagan authors in Latin and Greek.

To make the most of any library, an abbey such as Hilda's at Streanaeshalch would have needed some kind of scriptorium – a writing room – complete with desks, quill pens, ink and literate monks to act as scribes. These brothers would scratch away at copies of the texts that were already permanent fixtures in the library, or on loan to it so that they could be copied. There is no evidence of illuminated manuscripts being produced at Whitby, but if any were the scriptorium would also have had to be home to artist-monks, paints, brushes and quantities of gold leaf. Among the pigments used on the Lindisfarne Gospels were lapis lazuli, known to the ancient Egyptians and fetched from the far Himalayas.

Among Anglo-Saxon items dug up at Whitby are parts of the metal fittings of book-covers (like the clasp found by the *Time Team* people at Hartlepool), styluses for writing on wax tablets, and sharp prickers made from bone, used to mark out the pages of books that were in the process of being produced.

Though the educational programme at Streanaeshalch led to the conversion of many monks into priests, and contributed to the training of no fewer than five future bishops, it is possible that even by the time of Hilda's successor, Abbess Aelfflaed, educational standards at Streanaeshalch were somewhat less impressive than they were at Lindisfarne, over one hundred and thirty miles to the north. In the introduction to his edition of the aforementioned Whitby Life of Gregory the Great, Bertram Colgrave points out that the Latin of this book is very poor, and that the author had access to only a narrow range of sources. He or she may also have been quite ignorant of the Latin literature of the pagan Romans, written by such figures as Virgil, Ovid and Seneca.

A Latin Life of St Cuthbert, written around the same time on the island of Lindisfarne, is in much better Latin and shows knowledge of a wider range of authors. The Whitby writer did, however, have a good knowledge of the Bible, and access not only to the writings of his subject Gregory the great, but also the *Liber Pontificalis*, a set of biographies of popes that continued to be compiled until the fifteenth century. The author of the Whitby Life of Gregory may not have had to rely entirely on written sources, however. Paulinus had only died around sixty years before the anonymous Whitby author started his Life of Gregory. Paulinus had known Gregory and would no doubt have told his Anglo-Saxon converts stories about the great pope. The Whitby Life of Gregory is, therefore, in part an attempt to preserve in writing oral traditions about Gregory that were still current among the English in the early eighth century. Some of the stories related here are outlandish – were these embroidered by Anglo-Saxon story-tellers as they sat round their fires, yarning endlessly on winter nights?

Despite the limitations of the Whitby Life of Gregory, it and the anonymous Life of Cuthbert written on Lindisfarne may be the first extant writings known to have been produced by Anglo-Saxon authors. When a Roman called John the Deacon sat down to write his own biography of Gregory I in the 870s, the Whitby Life was one of the sources he used – a book written over thirteen hundred miles away, and over a century and a half earlier.

The Synod of Whitby

Though Hilda's abbey at Whitby may not have become the sort of university of Christianity that she might have wished to make it, a vital conference took place there in 664, which changed the future of Northumbria, and indeed the whole of England, and at which some genuine scholarship was exhibited. The synod had been called to thrash out a problem that had its roots in the odd way that the English had been converted to Christianity – from two different directions. In 635, Aidan's mission had brought Irish monks from Iona to the court of the Northumbrian King Oswald; but Augustine, sent by Pope Gregory the Great, had landed at Thanet nearly forty years earlier, and had proceeded to try to proselytise the people of Kent.

To make the picture even more complicated, the distant ancestors of many Celts living in Britain had been Christians in Roman times, and they maintained their old ways. And while Oswald had been a Celtic Christian, the earlier King Edwin of Northumbria had been converted by Paulinus, a friend of Pope Gregory and very much a Latin Christian. The disputants at the Synod of Whitby, that was attended by King

Oswiu himself, were tasked with airing the differences between the two churches, so that Oswiu could decide between them.

In the year of the conference, Hilda would have reached an age close to fifty: by this time, she had been abbess at Streanaeshalch, whether or not that was actually Whitby, for around seven years. Her ward Aelfflaed was perhaps ten years old. If Oswiu was not in the habit of regularly travelling the thirty or so miles from his base in Bernicia to visit his little daughter, then the synod of 664 may have seen a big reunion between father and daughter, with Aelfflaed's spiritual mother Hilda looking on.

Oswiu's use of Whitby Abbey as the venue for the great debate not only allowed him to visit his daughter; while he was there, he could also check on how Hilda was running the place, and also ensure, by his royal presence, that everybody remembered that the abbey was under his protection and control.

The major sticking-point, or perhaps symbolic point of conflict, between the Celts and the Romans at the Synod of Whitby was the calculation of the date of Easter, which is supposed to happen on the first Sunday after the so-called Paschal full moon, an event that relates to the date of the Jewish Passover. Readers familiar with the Gospels will know that Jesus was crucified, then rose again, after he had celebrated Passover with his disciples in the upper room of a building in Jerusalem (this was the so-called Last Supper). Easter celebrates his resurrection.

The Paschal full moon cannot happen on the same date every year in the Gregorian calendar (adopted by the British in 1752) because it is fixed to a date in a lunar calendar. There would be no problem if the earth would just speed up or slow down a little in its annual trek around the sun, so that every year was, say, exactly three hundred and sixty-five, or sixty-six, days long. If the moon could do likewise, the lunar calendar could line up properly with the likes of the Gregorian and Julian calendars.

In 2024, when the book you are reading was written, Roman Catholic Easter, which is shared by the Anglicans, Methodists and many others, fell on Sunday the thirty-first of March. By contrast, the Easter of those Orthodox churches that stick to the Julian calendar fell on Sunday the fifth of May, over a month later. The Catholic or Latin Easter, based on the Gregorian calendar, can never fall as late as May the fifth, but is restricted to Sundays between March the twenty-second and April the twenty-fifth. Last year (2023) the Easter recognised by most Brits happened on the ninth of April.

Today in the West we rely on calendars (whether in paper or electronic form) and to a lesser extent on newspapers, TV and radio to find out when Easter is going to be in a given year. This was not an option for Christians living over thirteen hundred years ago in remote parts of the world such as Ireland or the north of England. Some of them had to devise their own calendars, and calculate the correct date of Easter from scratch. There were different methods of doing this, one of which was devised by a third-century saint called Anatolius of Laodicea (now Latakia in Syria). Anatolius's method was preferred by the Celtic Christians in England, whereas the Latins adhered to the system devised by one Victorius of Aquitaine in the middle of the fifth century.

Discrepancies between the two systems had been causing problems at least as far back as the pontificate of Gregory the Great. Near the end of the sixth century, our friend the Irish saint Columbanus, founder of Celtic-style monasteries in Continental Europe, wrote a bold letter to Pope Gregory which opened with a section about the superiority of Anatolius's way. This method, the Irishman asserted, had the approval of St Jerome, whereas Victorius's way was not backed up by holy scripture, and caused ignorant Christians to endanger their very souls by celebrating Easter at a 'time of darkness'.

Perhaps, Columbanus suggested, Gregory was respectfully following the example of his predecessor Pope Leo I, who approved Victorius? Surely, Gregory's correspondent asserted, playing on Leo's name and alluding to a passage in the Old Testament Book of Ecclesiastes, a live dog is better than a dead lion? (Ecclesiastes 9,4). Despite the tetchiness that sometimes arose over this question (which is evident in Columbanus's letter) Bede tells us that in Northumbria during the time of Aidan a 'mixed' approach 'was patiently tolerated by all men'. Do we dare to suggest that Anglo-Saxon Christians in England were more concerned than some of their Celtic contemporaries about the correct calculation of Easter, because of the way their pagan ancestors had anxiously watched the phases of the moon, waiting for an auspicious time to hold certain meetings?

Every year, the way that Easter moves up and down the calendar seems to cause inconvenience, particularly for people working in education, where the years, terms and holidays are traditionally based around Christian festivals. The Easter problem, as we may term it, was compounded at the court of King Oswiu of Northumbria because in some years he, a Celtic Christian, was celebrating Easter when his wife Eanfled, a Latin Christian, was fasting for Lent. As we know, Eanfled went to live with her daughter Aelfflaed at the abbey at Whitby after she became a widow.

The climax of the Synod of Whitby was a showdown between Abbot (later bishop and saint) Wilfrid for the Roman side, and Colman, an Irishman and a Celtic-style Christian like Columbanus. Colman was the third bishop of Lindisfarne after Aidan, and his successor Finan, who had died in 661.

Defending the method his community used, Colman told the synod that all his 'forefathers, men beloved of God' had used his system, and that John the Evangelist had used the same system. This claim of Colman's was problematic: the system that was traditionally regarded as having been derived from the practice of John was used by Christians in Asia, whose Easter coincided with the date of the Jewish Passover, whether that happened on a Sunday or any other day of the week. Christians who followed this system were called 'Quartodecimans' in the Middle Ages, and were believed by many to be well and truly barking up the wrong tree. The name 'Quartodecimans', used by some as a term of abuse, was derived from the fact that the relevant believers celebrated Easter on the fourteenth day of the Jewish month of Nisan (which began on the ninth of April in 2024).

Asked to respond to Colman's assertions, Wilfrid led with what he had learned about Easter on his travels. Although he was only around thirty years old in 664, and lived at a time when travel was difficult, slow and full of dire risks, the young abbot had been to Rome, and may in fact have been among the first English people to make a pilgrimage to the Eternal City. On the way there, Wilfrid had also spent some time at Lyon.

Making the most of his status as a well-travelled individual, Wilfrid told the spectators at the Synod of Whitby that he had seen the Roman Easter being marked at Rome, in all Italy and in Gaul, and had:

. . . found it observed in Africa, Asia, Egypt, Greece, and all the world, wherever the Church of Christ is spread abroad, among divers nations and tongues, at one and the same time . . .

Now Wilfrid had not been far outside of Britain, Gaul and Italy, and it seems unlikely that anyone at this time could have known for sure that all the Christians living around the Mediterranean and beyond calculated the date of Easter in the same way, and celebrated the festival at the same time; but luckily for Wilfrid nobody laughed at his assertion. He wound up his first response to Colman by stating that only 'these and their accomplices in obstinacy, I mean the Picts and the Britons, who foolishly, in these two remote islands of the ocean, and only in part even of them, strive to oppose all the rest of the world'.

Responding to Wilfrid's scornful attack, Colman reminded the assembly that John the Evangelist, whom he believed had originated their system, had been the best-loved of the disciples of Jesus, 'who was thought worthy to lean on our Lord's bosom' and was known by everyone to have lived wisely.

Having first tried geography on Colman, Wilfrid now moved on to history. John the beloved disciple, he asserted, had stuck to the fourteenth of Nisan because at that time Christianity was still struggling to extricate itself from the Jewish beliefs of many of its first followers. By the time St Peter began to preach in Rome, the spiritual ancestor of the line of popes felt able to adapt John's system so that Easter could always be celebrated on a Sunday. Since Colman's people always kept Easter on a Sunday, they were neither following John's system, or Peter's.

In response, Colman put John the Evangelist aside and reminded his listeners of the holy reputation of Anatolius of Laodicea, who had formalised the system he used. In response to this, Wilfrid argued that as well as trampling all over the systems of John and Peter, the Celts did not follow Anatolius's method either! Yes, many of Colman's predecessors, who had followed his system, were holy men, Wilfrid agreed; but they would not have been so foolish as to have stuck to their erroneous system if they had been shown a better one.

In any case, Wilfrid concluded, even if St Columba, the Irish abbot who had founded the abbey on Iona and followed Colman's system, was indeed a very holy man, should his opinion be given more respect than that of Peter, of whom

Jesus said 'Thou art Peter, and upon this rock I will build my Church'? (Matthew 16:18).

This argument seemed to impress King Oswiu very much, and when he had asked some questions and got the ideas clear in his head, he announced his intention to embrace the Roman way.

Although the dispute at Whitby had been, on one level, to do with a trivial matter of dates and calendars, the argument had touched on some enduring Christian questions: the international nature of the Church, the supremacy of Rome as a spiritual centre, and the fact that Christianity itself had grown out of Jewish soil.

Wilfrid seemed to celebrate the fact that with Peter, the Jewish fisherman from Galilee who, according to legend, became the first Bishop of Rome and began the papal succession, Christianity finally broke free from Judaism. Such ideas, which can be found in the New Testament itself, are not unconnected to the persistent anti-Semitism that has accompanied Christianity like an ugly rash throughout much of its long history.

Though the account in the *Ecclesiastical History* would seem to suggest that Oswiu made up his mind to switch to the Roman side as soon as Wilfrid had finished speaking, it is possible that he had decided earlier, and that the debate that was set up on Hilda's home turf was little more than ceremonial. There were political as well as religious advantages for Oswiu in his choice: whereas before the synod, Bernicia had been Celtic and Deira Roman, if both were Roman it might be easier to rule the whole of Northumbria as a unified kingdom.

Hilda's abbey hosted this momentous synod, but there is no suggestion that either she or any other woman contributed to the debate. This contrasts oddly with Bede's insistence that Hilda was a woman of wisdom and experience, whose advice and opinions were eagerly sought out by the great and the good. Can it be that, like women down the ages, Hilda was obliged to work behind the scenes, influencing affairs through private conversations, instead of standing up and being heard in public?

Bede tells us that Hilda favoured the Celtic side, although she was related to King Edwin, and had been baptised with him by Paulinus at York. In any case she must have realised that, after the synod, the Church in her part of England was now more bound up with the Church in Rome than it had been before. Much of Britain would continue to be part of Latin Christendom until King Henry VIII's sixteenth-century Reformation.

However strongly Hilda held to her Celtic convictions, and however completely she yielded to the new Roman *status quo*, there seems to have been little love lost between the abbess and Wilfrid, who had proved to be such a formidable disputant in 664. According to Eddius Stephanus, the biographer of Wilfrid, when he returned to Rome years later to appeal to the pope for help in a dispute, representatives of Hilda were already there, ready to oppose him.

If Hilda regretted the decision arrived at at the momentous synod that happened under her roof, many of the faithful in modern times would sympathise with her. A considerable proportion of the most popular books on

Christianity published over recent years have been about Celtic Christianity, although as the authors of a 1995 anthology of Celtic Christian writings remind us, Colman and his companions would not have called themselves Celts.

In the introduction to their book *Celtic Christian Spirituality*, Oliver Davies and Fiona Bowie reflect on how many modern believers find the Celtic Christian tradition 'more ecological, imaginative, intuitive and theologically sound'. As a form of Christianity that stood out against the internationalism of the Roman way, the Celtic way can also seem more home-grown, especially from the point of view of people with Celtic ancestry.

Later medieval ruins at Whitby.

The Last of Hilda

Bede is clear that Hilda suffered from a fever for six years, *i.e.* from around the year 674 CE: her fever ultimately 'turned inward' and killed her. Likely candidates for this mysterious disease include tuberculosis, which modern people tend to associate with Victorian slums, but which has been with us for thousands of years, and has by no means gone away. A nineteenth-century examination of St Cuthbert's bones raised the possibility that that beloved saint had also suffered from TB. Certainly he seems to have had a deep-seated illness that got better and worse at various times, and may ultimately have killed him when he was only in his fifties.

Although we tend to think of TB as a respiratory problem, in can effect other parts of the body, including the bones and skin. Scrofula, a tubercular infection of the skin, used to be called 'the king's evil' in England because it was believed that it could clear up if the area affected was touched by the reigning monarch. The tradition was started by the saintly King Edward the Confessor, the penultimate Anglo-Saxon king of the English, who died in 1066.

As what the Victorians called a 'consumptive', Hilda may have suffered from a persistent, perhaps bloody, cough, fever, fatigue and a loss of appetite. Bede does not mention a cough, which makes it more likely that the saint's fever was caused by something other than TB. A candidate that may surprise some readers is malaria: marshes like Hatfield Chase, where King Edwin died in battle, were just the kinds of wetland habitats where malaria-bearing mosquitoes could thrive. Hilda would only have needed to travel through or near such a place once to have contracted malaria. Today anyone suffering from malaria in England would have brought it back from overseas: not so in the seventh century. In fact the last outbreak where the patients affected are known to have caught malaria in Britain itself ended in 1921.

We can get some idea of what life was like in the marshlands from the biography of the fenland saint, Guthlac of Crowland, a younger contemporary of Hilda. Felix, the eighth-century author of the Latin *Vita sancti Guthlaci*, tells us that after some time spent in a monastery, Guthlac sought a hermit's life in a part of the wetlands that many considered to be uninhabitable:

There is in Britain a fen of immense size, which begins from the river Granta not far from the city, which is named Grantchester. There are immense marshes, now a black pool of water, now foul running streams, and also many islands, and reeds, and hillocks, and thickets, and with manifold windings wide and long it continues up to the north sea. When the aforesaid man, Guthlac of blessed memory, found out this uncultivated spot of the wide wilderness, he was comforted with divine support, and journeyed forthwith by the straightest way thither.

(trans. C.W. Goodwin, 1848)

Guthlac is supposed to have been visited by many demons during his time on his island in the fens, which human beings could only reach by boat. It may be that he had contracted malaria, and was having hallucinations because of the fever that is a symptom of the disease.

In the same way that Guthlac relished living in such a dreadful place, saintly patients like Hilda welcomed their various bodily afflictions. Ethelthryth, the chaste queen who took to the cloister while her husband King Egfrid was still alive, was long tormented by a painful tumour under her jaw. Perversely, she rejoiced in the 'fiery heat' of this, as she saw it as a punishment for the necklaces she had worn as a frivolous young girl. Despite the fact that she valued her tumour so much, Ethelthryth did eventually allow a physician called Cynifrid to lance it. The resulting wound was found to have healed after Ethelthryth's death.

Just like Ethelthryth, Hilda suffered her affliction with saintly patience, and continued her routine of praying, teaching and leading by example. Near dawn on the seventeenth of November 680, she died, having first called all her nuns together and 'admonished them to preserve the peace of the Gospel among themselves, and with all others'. She was sixty-six, a grand old age for an Anglo-Saxon lady.

When Aidan had died, St Cuthbert, who was then not yet a monk, is said to have seen his soul rise up to heaven. Hilda's ascension 'attended and guided by angels' is supposed to have been seen by a nun called Begu at Hackness, a recently-built cell or offshoot of Whitby's abbey.

A nun at Hilda's own abbey is supposed to have seen exactly the same thing at the same time.

Hilda was buried at Whitby, with Oswiu and Edwin, but her bones may later have been translated to a monument or 'pyramid' near the high altar of the church at Glastonbury Abbey. Since the abbeys of both Glastonbury and Whitby lie in ruins, nobody can say for sure where Hilda lies now.

The ruins that now dominate Whitby date from long after Hilda's time, but between 1920 and 1925 the stone outlines of a range of earlier buildings were uncovered to the north and south of the later ruins. These were not investigated using very scientific methods, but it may be judged from the surviving plans that at least some of the wooden buildings that stood on stone 'footings' were later replaced by structures with more stone in them.

The 1920s excavators, and others who worked later, discovered a number of artefacts that may relate to Hilda's abbey at Whitby. As well as the loom-weights and book-related artefacts already mentioned, there were carved stones, including one that may have been part of some sort of memorial to Aelfflaed. There were also tweezers, brooches, combs, crucifixes fashioned from the celebrated local jet, pottery, and coins dating from the end of the eighth century to the middle of the ninth. The most interesting find is a lead bulla or seal, evidently from a long-lost document sent to Whitby by an Archdeacon Boniface, from Rome, some time late in the seventh century.

Although the Anglo-Saxon finds at Whitby were plentiful, the written records that can be drawn on for a biography of Hilda are scanty. In a chapter of the 1999 book

Northumbria's Golden Age, Catherine Karkov suggests that Bede, almost our only source, may even have suppressed some information on Hilda, or down-played her importance. As we have seen, this possibility was also explored by Stephanie Hollis in her 1992 book *Anglo-Saxon Women and the Church*. Certainly, the only miracle Bede connects with Hilda is the vision that was granted simultaneously to two nuns in separate locations of her soul ascending to heaven. This, her mother's dream of the necklace, and Caedmon's sudden ability to compose verse, hardly count as miracles Hilda herself performed.

By contrast, the chronicler makes much more of Aelfflaed, once Hilda's ward, who also appears in his prose Life of St Cuthbert. It may be that the author of the *Ecclesiastical History* did not want to make too much of a woman who, unlike Aelfflaed, did not dedicate her whole life to the church, and may not have died a virgin.

Bede may also have disapproved of Hilda's preference for the Celtic way of doing things, and may have felt obliged to pay more attention to saintly contemporaries who were rather more aristocratic than she was. She was, after all, only the great-niece of a king, whereas Aelfflaed was a king's daughter, and other saints Bede writes about were themselves kings, queens, bishops or priests.

The author of the *Ecclesiastical History*, who may have struggled to find material about Hilda, was certainly clear that she was a very pious and capable woman, able to act as a good and faithful religious leader even during the years when she was suffering badly from the disease that ended her life. Aidan relied on Hilda to bring order to one monastery that may have been struggling, and to found or at least run two more. Like the wise women who lived among the Anglo-Saxons' pagan ancestors, Hilda found herself being consulted by powerful people on all sorts of matters. Such was her reach that she could even send representatives to Rome to convey her own thoughts about the troublesome St Wilfrid.

In a sermon preached in Hartlepool in 1885, the Victorian Bishop of Durham Joseph Lightfoot heaped praise on Hilda, comparing her to the Old Testament heroine Deborah, and Joan of Arc, and going on to say that the abbess was 'a chief maker of England'. In terms that are even more powerful because they are rather more subdued, the twentieth-century historian Frank Stenton wrote in his 1947 book *Anglo-Saxon England*, 'No woman in the middle ages ever held a position comparable to that of Hild of Whitby'.

Hilda on the memorial at Whitby.

Bibliography

Barmby, J., *Gregory the Great*, Pott, Young & Co., 1879

Bede (trans. Sellar, A.M.: *Bede's Ecclesiastical History of England*, George Bell & Sons, 1907

Bede (trans. Colgrave): *An Ecclesiastical History of the English People*, Oxford, 1999

Bentley, W: *The Story of the Abbey Church of St Hilda, Hartlepool*, British Publishing Company, 1960

Boenig, R, *Anglo-Saxon Spirituality*, Paulist, 2000

Carver, Martin (ed.): *The Cross Goes North*, York Medievalist Press, 2004

Colgrave, Bertram (ed.): *The Earliest Life of Gregory the Great by an Anonymous Monk of Whitby*, University of Kansas Press, 1968

Colgrave, Bertram: *Two Lives of St Cuthbert*, Cambridge, 1985

Daniels, Robin: *Hartlepool, an Archaeology of the Medieval Town*, Tees Archaeology, 2010

Davies, Oliver and Bowie, Fiona: *Celtic Christian Spirituality*, SPCK, 1995

Davies, Owen, *Paganism*, Oxford, 2011

Felix of Crowland (trans. Goodwin, C.W.): *The Anglo-Saxon Version of the Life of St. Guthlac*, John Russell Smith, 1848

Gildas and Nennius (trans. J.A. Giles): *The Works of Gildas and Nennius*, Bohn, 1881

Glasswell, Samantha: *The Earliest English: Living & Dying in Early Anglo-Saxon England*, Tempus, 2002

Gregorovius, Ferdinand (trans. Hamilton, Annie): *A History of the City of Rome in the Middle Ages*, George Bell & Sons, 1894

Hamer, Richard: *A Choice of Anglo-Saxon Verse*, Faber, 1970

Hawkes, Jane and Mills, Susan: *Northumbria's Golden Age*, Sutton, 1999

Heaney, Seamus: *Beowulf, a Verse Translation*, Norton, 2002

Hegge, Robert: *The Legend of St Cuthbert*, Langley Press, 2016

Herzfeld, George: *An Old English Martyrology*, Kegan Paul, Trench & Trübner, 1900

Hollis, Stephanie: *Anglo-Saxon Women and the Church: Sharing a Common Fate*, Boydell, 1992

Hunter-Blair, Peter: *An Introduction to Anglo-Saxon England*, Cambridge, 1959

Jonas (trans. Munro, D.C.: *The Life of St Columban*, University of Philadelphia, 1895

Lavelle, Ryan: *Alfred's Wars: Anglo-Saxon Warfare in the Viking Age*, Boydell, 2010

Lightfoot, Joseph Barber: *Leaders in the Northern Church*, Macmillan, 1892

Markus, R.A.: *Gregory the Great and His World*, Cambridge, 1997

Mayr-Harting, Henry: *The Coming of Christianity to Anglo-Saxon England*, Book Club Associates, 1977

Nicolle, David: *Arthur and the Anglo-Saxon Wars*, Osprey, 1984

Ramirez, Janina: *The Private Lives of the Saints*, WH Allen, 2023

Sharp, Cuthbert: *History of Hartlepool*, Hartlepool Borough Council, 1978

Stenton, Frank: *Anglo-Saxon England*, Oxford, 1989

Tacitus (trans. Mattingly, H.): *On Britain and Germany*, Penguin, 1948

Thomas, Gwyn (trans.): *Gododdin: The Earliest British Literature*, Gomer, 2012

Virgin Saints of the Benedictine Order, C.T.S., 1903

Webb, J.F. and Farmer, D.H. (trans.): *The Age of Bede*, Penguin, 1998

Webb, Simon: *In Search of Bede*, Langley Press, 2010

White, Andrew: *A History of Whitby*, Phillimore, 1993

Wright, J. Robert: *A Companion to Bede*, Eerdmans, 2008

For more from the Langley Press, please visit our website at:

www.langleypress.co.uk

Printed in Dunstable, United Kingdom

64060834R00058